THE ESKIMO GIRL AND THE ENGLISHMAN

This book is dedicated to my father and mother, who taught me honesty, truth, and appreciation of the many wonders of nature in this beautiful land.

The Eskimo Girl and the Englishman

Edna Wilder

UNIVERSITY OF ALASKA PRESS

Fairbanks

University of Alaska Press
PO Box 756240
Fairbanks, AK 99775-6240

The publication was printed on paper that meets the minimum requirements
for ANSI / NISO Z39.48–1992 (R2002).

Library of Congress Cataloging-in-Publication Data

Wilder, Edna, 1916–
The Eskimo girl and the Englishman / Edna Wilder.
 p. cm.
Includes bibliographical references and index.
ISBN-13: 978-1-60223-015-6 (pbk. : alk. paper)
ISBN-10: 1-60223-015-3 (pbk. : alk. paper)
1. Tucker, Minnie, ca. 1858-1979. 2. Eskimos—Alaska—Biography.
3. Eskimos—Alaska—Social life and customs. I. Title.
E99.E7T837 2008
305.897'1092—dc22
[B]
     2007023870

Interior Design by Rachel Fudge
Cover Design by Dixon Jones

Cover Image: White Mountain. Archives and Special Collections Department,
Consortium Library, of the University of Alaska Anchorage

Contents

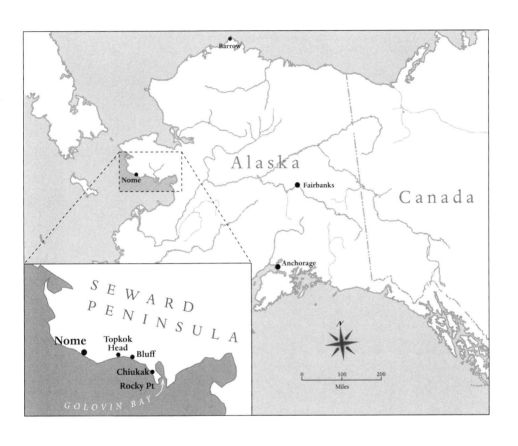

Barrow

Alaska

Fairbanks

Canada

Nome

Anchorage

S E W A R D
P E N I N S U L A

Nome
Topkok
Head
Bluff
Chiukak
Rocky Pt
GOLOVIN BAY

N

0   100   200
Miles

Acknowledgments

If it was not for the lifesaving care of doctor David S. Grauman M.D., and his encouraging words when I was undecided about writing the life of my parents, this book would not have been written.

A special thank you to William G. Stroecker for writing the foreword to this book. Carl Olson and Virginia Bedford contributed invaluable technical computer assistance. Ingrid Taylor helped with the manuscript. Snow or cold was not an obstacle for her! She was always careful not to change what she called "my style."

Some of the photographs were taken by Bunny Fuller, Helen Atkinson-Frank, and the late Professor Jimmy Bedford. Some are so old that I do not know the photographer's name. Our late friend Jerome E. Lardy did an excellent job of photography and printing for me over the years. I took the rest of the photographs.

Others who helped in a variety of ways that I will not detail here are: Alaska Link, Robert and Antonia Wilder, Charles J. Keim, Harry Olson, and others who wrote words of encouragement or called from out of state. Last but not least, for his patience and assistance, my husband Alex (AL7EX), and for faithful Tofty, who is always on guard.

To each of you, I wish to extend my sincere thanks and gratitude for your help.

Foreword

When *Edna Wilder asked me* to write the foreword to this book I was pleased. Our friendship goes back many years. In the early 1960s we belonged to the Fairbanks Retriever Club, and for several years I was president and she was the secretary and treasurer (she did most of the work). We both still have our black Labrador retrievers.

Then I acquired some of her artwork, including a beautiful oil painting of Mt. McKinley (Denali) done in 1962, and some soapstone carvings. Most prominent of her classic soapstone sculptures is the first ptarmigan she carved while taking a course in sculpture at the University of Alaska Fairbanks. That soapstone ptarmigan was presented to Senator Bob Bartlett by the University of Alaska School of Art in 1964. In 1977 a magazine article titled "She Frees the Birds" featured Edna sculpting in both soapstone and wood.

Her first writings were under her maiden name of Edna Tucker while she was living near the little mining town of Bluff, Alaska, located on the shore of the Bering Sea about sixty-five miles east of Nome. In Fairbanks, she took a course in journalism at the University of Alaska given by the late Charles J. Keim and Professor Jimmy Bedford. She wrote her first book, *Secrets of Eskimo Skin Sewing*, which is widely distributed and is used as a textbook not only in Alaska but elsewhere.

Edna's second book, *Once Upon an Eskimo Time*, relates experiences of her mother Minnie (Nedercook) as a girl before the coming of the white man. Minnie was living in the Eskimo village of Rocky Point, located on the shore of Norton Sound east of Bluff. Wayne Mergler included a chapter from this book called "Eggs" in his book *The Last New Land*, an anthology of Alaska literature.

This third book is about her mother Minnie, the "Eskimo Girl," and her father Sam Tucker, the "Englishman." It tells the story of Minnie's life, which extended to over a century, and that of Sam from his crossing the Chilkoot Pass and rafting the Yukon River, and his married life with Minnie on the Seward Peninsula. It describes the hardships and tragedies of those living in that isolated region in a vivid way. This book is unique because of Minnie's long life and her recollections. Her desire to record their history fits in perfectly with Edna's ability to write. The grit and determination of Sam and Minnie are reflected in the success of their daughter in overcoming the obstacles in her own life.

Bill Stroecker

1

Sammy-Sis-Co

In this land of peace with nature Nedercook had knowledge only of the natives of Alaska between the villages of Cape Nome and Fish River. There were no mechanical sounds, only the sounds of her people, dogs, wild birds and animals, storms, wind, and rain. Possibly once or twice a year in summer, there was thunder. The songs of her people and those of the wild birds were the only musical sounds she heard. Knowing no other life, she was happy with hers. Looking out across the Bering Sea she would wonder if on the other side of this big salty lake other people were living too.

As she grew older she would look toward Rocky Point and imagine the day to come when she would be old enough that her father would take her to the top of the tallest part of the mountain, called Iknutak. Others who had been there said that near the top was a circle of very old driftwood, like a circle that would form if that was the only piece of land above water. In places above this circle there were the remains of very old shelters. The wood, it was said, looked very old. Nedercook was curious, and she wanted to see this. Caribou roamed the mountain during this period, and in the spring the bowhead whales would pass near Rocky Point. She remembered times when the water in Golovin Bay looked as if it were solid with the heads of passing walrus, but they too became scarce and had all but disappeared by the time Nedercook became a woman.

On a sunny but chilly day when Nedercook was in her early teens, she gathered together her bow, arrows, ulu (Eskimo knife), and pack sack, which was made from a seal hide and had one strap that passed over the shoulder. Then she went walking out across the tundra as she had learned to do in childhood, always in search of anything edible. She spotted a large flock of ptarmigan. Now their feathers were white in preparation for the coming winter snow. All stood white against the dark tundra. Staying downwind from them she decided to creep close enough for a shot with her bow and arrow, careful not to make any quick moves but still staying on the lookout for danger. Her eye caught a movement to her right, and she saw what appeared to be a person. Her body became tense. She had never seen anyone who looked like what was coming toward her—even the way it walked seemed different to her.

What shall I do? wondered Nedercook, as she lay huddled in the grass. The strangely dressed person kept coming in a line that would bring him to her. She was sure that he had not seen her yet, but in a little while he would. Fear got the better of her when the hairs on the back of her neck seemed to stand up. Clutching her bow and arrow tightly, she came to her feet running, scaring the ptarmigan to flight. With the movement the stranger saw her. He stopped. She heard him yell strange sounds that were foreign to her ears. They sounded like "Stop…Hey…stop!" These strange noises made no sense to her—if anything, they made her legs go faster as she ran like she never had before. Rushing into the inne she found her father working on some damaged hunting equipment.

"Stranger coming," she gasped, then could not speak until she had some water. Her father, Inerluk, got up and after more questions and answers told Nedercook and her mother to stay there as he went outdoors. Soon voices were heard, as Inerluk and the stranger started to come down the steps to the inne. Nedercook was so frightened by now that she crawled under her bedding and hid. The stranger made many sounds that Nedercook did not understand. The word "San Francisco" was repeated a few times, and if she had been brave enough to look out, she would have seen the stranger place his hand on his chest and say, "I am from San Francisco." None of it made any sense to anyone. Inerluk tried to communicate with him, but it was no use. Nedercook's mother, Kiachook, thought he might be hungry and offered him a bowl of food. He gratefully took it, smiled at the faces around him, and began to eat. He was very hungry.

When the man finished eating, Inerluk told the villagers to take him to the Big Dance Hall, a large underground dwelling used for visitors, where unmarried men slept, and live coals were always kept glowing and ready for anyone who needed a fire. (There was a side room used as a sauna, and small storage rooms were dug into the dirt wall of the passageway.)

Hearing the man repeat "San Francisco" so often, the villagers, for lack of a better name, decided to call him "Sammy-sis-co." He had light brown hair and was dressed in strange clothes that were not made of skin. Later, when it became apparent that he could not survive outdoors in his strange worn-out clothes, the elders decided that an outfit of clothes like they wore should be made and given to him, because although they could not converse with him, he always tried to help and did his share of the work. He was not a good hunter but he was learning to throw the spear and shoot the arrow.

Life in the village soon returned to normal. One day when Nedercook's brothers were away and her parents were not at home, she completed the grass rug that she had been working on, then came out of the inne to see snow falling. It was the beginning of winter and it looked like a real storm was brewing. Nedercook was always active and today she was feeling stronger than her years. She decided to carry in some of the foodstuff that was usually stored indoors for the winter. Hoping to surprise her parents, she made several trips. She was too busy to notice that the snow from her mukluk soles was slowly forming a thin sheet of ice on the top steps. *I can carry that*, she thought as she looked at the heavy seal poke, which was filed with partially dried seal meat and oil. It was heavy and awkward, but she was determined to get it onto her shoulder. She walked with a staggering movement under the weight until she reached the top step. Moving to lower herself to the next step, she felt herself slipping and the heavy seal poke started to tip. In an effort to correct it, she fell tumbling down the steps. The heavy seal poke came crashing down upon her and rolled to the side. Nedercook was frightened as she lay there because she had never felt like that before. When she tried, she could not get up. She cried out in pain and called for help, but there was no one there. Her mother was in the village helping a woman who had hurt herself, both brothers were away hunting, and her father was fishing some distance up the coast. She lay helpless on the floor as the world outside became darker.

Her father was the first to find her. He saw the seal poke and knew that she was badly hurt. He quickly climbed the steps and called for someone to bring the Miracle Man right away. With his sensitive fingers the Miracle Man moved his hands over her back.

"Broken," he said as he raised his eyes to her father. By then Kiachook had returned, and with her help the Miracle Man took some of the pieces of flatter wood that her father had made in hopes of a new sled and placed some along her back and some in front. Then all were bound in place with thin rawhide.

"This must stay on for a long time," he said, "maybe three or four moons, maybe longer. We can only wait and see."

"And if not?" Nedercook asked weakly.

"If you take the wood off too soon you will always look like a cripple...bent and stooped," he replied. As uncomfortable as it was,

Nedercook thought, *I'll live with the wood until I am well.* As the darker days of winter approached, her family did all they could for her because she could not even turn over without their help. Even with the soft fur between her body and the hard wood pressing on her, each day seemed like an eternity. She thought over and over again, *If I had not wanted to test my strength so much, I could be outdoors walking, running, hunting.*

She did not see much of Sammy-sis-co, but he came to see her several times. He tried to teach her some of his words. He never stayed long. She could sense that he felt sorry for her. From other women, she heard accounts of his life in the village and also of a song that one of the women had composed. Her sister learned the song and taught it to her. Although she could not sing very well while lying strapped up like she was, she learned the words and was able to sing the song later, remembering it for life.

With the coming of spring Sammy-sis-co made it known that he intended to leave. He would go west along the coast. For his trip Inerluk gave him some dried salmon, meat, and a fur robe. Nedercook's sister Paniagon told of his leaving on foot early one morning. As the villagers watched he turned and waved before going over the ridge and out of sight. He was never seen again.

While Nedercook was recovering from her fall her brother Oolark got married. How she had wanted to go to the Big Dance Hall to see the elders speak of this marriage!

After winter, when food became plentiful, Minnie's people had a big celebration lasting for days until the food was gone. Village people provided food for everyone, including visitors. Presents were exchanged and dancing was popular. They called it the Big Festival. When it was time for the Big Festival she wanted so much to be able to attend. She asked the Miracle Man if her brothers could carry her. His answer was a firm "No," but then he added more kindly, "If you want to get well, you stay."

That winter seemed like it would never end for Nedercook. Just when she thought it would not, she noticed that the skylight was letting in more light that stayed longer each day.

As the daylight increased, Nedercook eagerly watched from her bed as each day brought more light to the skylight opening. How she longed for the wood to be removed from her body. Her family spoke encouraging words, even after the visits of the Miracle Man, and the wood remained on her body. One day the Miracle Man came and carefully moved his fingers around her back.

"We take wood off today, but you must be very careful, no fast moves and no walking today," he cautioned.

With the thought of going out and roaming the hills again, Nedercook's heart was filled with joy. When the last piece of wood was removed from her body she planned to jump up and go outside ... but she was too weak, because the many days of inactivity had taken their toll. She burst into tears. Kiachook, who was ever near, took her hands and explained the cause of her weakness. Slowly she would have to build back her strength, and after much trial and effort she would walk and run again. But not now ... For now, her mother said, it was enough that the hard wood was gone from her body.

Early the next morning a woman came to Inerluk's home. She believed that draining away the old blood from one's body would speed up the recovery. She brought with her a pointed tool, and with it she stabbed Nedercook several times around her knees and a few times in the back. This was painful and the loss of blood made Nedercook even weaker. The scars around her knees were visible until her death. The days of spring brought more and more light, and with it Nedercook's strength grew. Every day she could move a little more. Slowly she made it across the floor and back to her bed, until one day she finally reached the bottom of the steps where she had fallen. Kiachook went up and opened the heavy skins, and there was the beautiful blue sky.

One afternoon she made it to the top of the steps. As she sat on a skin outside the entranceway, gazing out over the village and across the Bering Sea, her heart was so full of joy that tears filled her eyes. From that day on she improved more rapidly. Soon she could go up the steps and even walk a little. One day she made it to the little knoll above the inne. Pale and thin in her parka-clad body, she sat and absorbed the sun, felt the caressing breeze of spring, and her heart was thankful. She stayed until her mother came and said, "Let's go eat."

By fall she was walking quite well but she was cautious as she descended the steps. By the next summer she could run again—not as fast as before—but she could run. Now she could take up her bow and arrow. Her brothers had made a new one, bigger and more suitable for her age.

Occasionally visiting natives would come to the village and tell of people who came from Siberia who brought a little tea and tobacco for trade. It was always very costly, they said, because it came from white people who lived very far away. One day a small boat with two traders came and stopped at the village. When Nedercook saw them coming she was so afraid that she hid under her bedding. They spoke very badly pronounced Eskimo and some English. When they saw the beautiful grass rug that Nedercook had finished just before she fell and broke her back, they wanted it. Her rug was traded for some plug tobacco and a few loose dry leaves. The traders left to barter with the village people, and Nedercook joined her parents and she also took a small chew from the plug tobacco.

2

Oolark's Last Hunt

Just *before the blueberry season* Oolark's wife gave birth to a baby boy, which brought much joy to the Inerluk family. Rocky Point Eskimos treated their babies very well.

As fall approached, life around the village was busy with preparations for the winter. It was the women's responsibility during the year to gather small pieces of wood that needed no cutting for the indoor cook fires, enough to last through the long winter days. This year Nedercook took over the job from her mother, but whenever Kiachook happened to be on the beach she would carry a few pieces of the small wood home. While Nedercook was wandering the beaches, as she often did after a storm, she found a large bow in good shape. She took it back home and gave it to her brother Oolark.

The cold days of winter arrived, bringing winds from the north, freezing the ground, lakes, streams, and the water on the Bering Sea. Occasionally, on calm sunny days, a seal would surface on the sea-ice to have a last sleep and rest before the dark days of winter. These seals were not as relaxed as those that lay on top of the ice during the warm days of spring.

One day such a seal appeared on the ice in front of the village. It showed up dark against a new covering of snow that had fallen during the night.

Oolark, who had spotted the seal, decided he would try to get it. After he reached the sea ice he traveled quite fast because the seal was hidden by a small pressure ridge which he had noted before he left the village. This would be a treat if he could get it. Since the ice had frozen over, the only fresh meat was an occasional ptarmigan. He hurried on, hoping the seal would still be there. The new snow made the slick spots slippery. In his excitement to get the seal he did not pay much attention to this. Stepping in the soft snow seemed a quiet way to go. When he crossed over the pressure ridge he tried to keep his eye on the seal while moving forward quickly so he could stop before it raised its head.

All the villagers were watching, wondering if Oolark would be lucky. Suddenly, while he was rushing forward they saw him disappearing down, an involuntary movement raising his right arm as he sank. To the onlookers it seemed to convey a final farewell.

Villagers hurried out to where he was last seen. His tracks ended by an open hole full of water, but they could not see him. Quick thinkers had brought with them the hook that was used to drag for seal or beluga whale when occasionally a dead one would sink before it could be retrieved.

Inerluk and others stationed themselves around the hole and tried for hours to catch something with the hook. Before dark the Miracle Man came down and, seeing how tired and grieved Inerluk was, he asked to take Inerluk's hook. Nedercook did not remember how long it was—perhaps an hour or more—before the Miracle Man's hook caught something, and he carefully pulled. He had hooked onto Oolark's mukluk. Quickly, many hands reached for him and he was pulled from the water. He was carried to Inerluk's home. His damp clothing was removed and replaced by dry ones, but it was of no use. His hands and feet had already become stiff and hard. He was dead.

The loss of this son hurt Inerluk very deeply. His grief was evident to all who saw him. Sorrow showed on the face of Oolark's young wife as she clung to their little boy. Nedercook and her mother could not hold back their tears.

Winter passed. Inerluk tried hard to put this sorrow behind him, but anyone who knew him could see what it cost. Nedercook kept the silent grief in her heart. Seeing the pain in her father's face was hard to bear. She would try her best to help him face each day. Kiachook did what she could, but she knew her husband's grief, like her own, was still deep.

The salmon run for the season would soon start. It was most important that the villagers be ready to put up as much as they could, because salmon was one of their main food items for the winter. The move to the summer camp by the clear running stream seemed to help Inerluk.

3

Dreadful Illness

One afternoon *Nedercook and a girl* about her own age were wandering around on the tundra to see if the salmonberries might be ripe. Suddenly Nedercook heard quite plainly the sounds of a really sick person. They could see no one, but to Nedercook the sounds seemed to be coming toward them. Her friend saw the fright on Nedercook's face and panicked. Both ran for home. Later a meeting was called by the Miracle Man. When the villagers had gathered on the beach he announced, "There is a bad sickness, I see it coming to our people."

A few days later in the afternoon, three white traders came in a small boat and landed near the summer camp. With much arm waving and some poorly spoken native words mixed with English they were able to make many exchanges. The traders then returned to their beached boat, and over a campfire cooked and ate before leaving.

Nedercook waited until the traders were well on their way, then she went to get a bucket of fresh water. She walked down to where the traders had been. Something near the water's edge caught her eye. Quickly she ran to it and found three enamel plates. Apparently the men had forgotten to pick them up, or perhaps they had fallen from the overloaded boat while the men were busy launching it. These were her first white man's treasures. Proudly carrying them, she ran back to her parents' shelter.

After this, life resumed as usual, women recalling the things the traders did and discussing their looks. Time passed, possibly a week or more. Suddenly the villagers began to feel sick and their skin became marked with rashes and red spots. The sickness was unlike any these people had known. It brought down the old, the young, and the strong hunters of the village. Overnight, it seemed to Neder-cook, everyone was sick and weak. She was the only one who still had the strength to carry water. Her father and all her family lay helpless inside their shelter. All wanted water. From nearby Ringley Creek she carried water to them. Soon she could hear the cries from other shelters.

"Water, I need water, bring me some water!" The cries seemed to come from every shelter.

"Water, I need water, bring me some water!" or "Help . . . I am thirsty. . . . Water, I need water!" They sounded so desperate. Neder-cook carried water with her buckets and left filled containers within reach of the sick as she moved from shelter to shelter. She carried water through the day, and because it was summer when the nights never got dark, she carried water through much of the night too. She was tired but the cries of the children, the elderly, and the men who only yester-day it seemed were strong but now lay helpless kept her going.

For days—she did not remember for how long—water was all they called for and Nedercook carried it. She did not keep track of time but just kept on answering the cries for help.

Her father worried her the most because he was having such a hard time. When he became too weak to lift the cup of water she would hold it to his lips. He managed a weak smile each time. Once he reached out and lightly patted her hand while she held the cup. In a weak, fal-

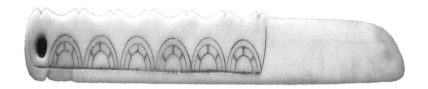

An ivory crimping knife made by Inerluk. It is used for pushing in the crimp-ing on hard oogruk (seal) skin mukluk soles. Photo by Jerome E. Lardy.

tering voice he managed to slowly say, "You are...caring...for our...-people...my girl...be...strong."

The shelters were spread out, and Nedercook would get so tired and sleepy that at times she would stop to rest and fall asleep. Waking, she would hear the weak cries and moans of her people. As more and more were dying in their shelters, she thought they must have food to get better.

As if to answer her thoughts, the salmon were jumping from the sea in a silvery flash—the long-awaited salmon run was on. She remembered the net. Wearily she walked to get the long pole. Her father had made it by taking several of the same size poles, placing the two tapered ends one above the other, and binding them securely together. He used this for years to push his net into the water. She was thankful the pole and net were just above the high-water line where he had left them when he began to feel ill. It was an effort to pull it to the water's edge, then an even greater struggle to drag the heavy net, lay it out beside the pole, and hook the outer end over the notch at the end of the pole. The thought of bringing strength back to her people gave her the will to carry on. With one hand she held onto the net like her father did. As she pushed the pole out into the water with her other hand, the pole took the net along with it. At last it was out far enough to let the net rope go. With both hands on the pole she gave it a push, followed by a sudden yank back on the pole. This freed the net from the notch on the end of the pole, but the sudden action caused her to stumble back and fall. It was hard for her to pull the pole back up above the high-water line.

She went to the outdoor fireplace and added more wood. Then she filled some pots partway with water and, as her mother had taught her, she added some of the salty seawater before putting them to heat. She hardly knew day from night, but it did not matter, if only she could have the strength to continue. She made more trips with water. When she reached her shelter, her father lay so quietly. Frightened, she knelt beside him to check his breathing. It was weak.

She went to the beach, but had no idea how long the net was set—possibly an hour or so. Now she must pull the net in by herself. The expectation of catching some fish gave her added strength, and she pulled hard on the net. Salmon were in the net flopping about. She knew that she could not run and catch those that became free from the net. She decided to just pull and pull until all the net was out of the water and up on dry land. Then she killed the salmon as quickly as she could, because she had been taught never to let anything she caught suffer.

Carrying the fish up the beach and to the fire was a chore, but knowing that she was bringing strength to her people was enough to keep her going. She cut the fish in smaller than usual pieces, so cooking would be quicker and the broth would be richer. When the first pot was cooked she set it aside and replaced it with another. Then she began the hard task of carrying the pots to the sick. Starting with the nearest and working her way slowly from shelter to shelter, she felt an inner satisfaction because she was helping her people.

Many were still too weak and sick to even try to take a swallow. In her rounds she noticed that some had taken the long sleep since she was last there. Entering her father's shelter she carefully put the steaming pot down near her mother, turning to look at her father. He was so still. She knew, before going to him, that he too had joined those of the long sleep. Kneeling by him, she remembered his last words, "My girl...be...strong." They seemed to run over and over in her mind. As the tears fell fast she thought, *For you Papa...I will be strong.*

Her mother was still too weak to sit up, so Nedercook helped her hold the cup while she slowly sipped the broth. "Daughter, you are helping us...keep strong." Exhausted, she closed her eyes as she lay back. For a moment Nedercook felt panic as she thought that her mother too had joined her father, but then she noticed the rise and fall of her mother's chest. Nedercook worked in a daze for the rest of the day, tired and numb with pain, as her father's words kept running through her mind while she carried pot after pot of fish and broth to the other shelters. More and more were now eager to get nourishment and it cheered her. One was her best friend, a girl about her own age. "Get well and help me," Nedercook whispered to her.

The dead were now becoming bloated and the smell of death was everywhere. Nedercook had no time and no strength to move the bodies—carrying water and preparing fish took it all. Tired, she sat on a log. She looked up at the sky and wondered, *Will there ever be an end to this...and where are you Papa?* Then came oblivion. Later she became aware that she was lying beside the log and the sun was shining on her as it came up over the horizon. She stirred and felt stiff as she realized that she had slept through the night. Going to her father's shelter, she found her mother strong enough to sit up. She went into her arms and together they wept. Finally her mother released her and asked, "Our people?"

"Many have left us and sleep the long sleep." Then Nedercook added, "Some are getting well, and I am sure my best friend will be walking today." Her friend recovered fast and Nedercook was glad to have her help and company. Next day the two went to a nearby salmonberry patch and picked some, giving a few to those who could eat. Some of the young men recovered enough to move about. Soon they were helping with the net and the packing of fish. Nedercook smiled for the first time in weeks as she looked at the life that now stirred outside of the shelters. She knew that her lonely days of work were over as more and more recovered. It saddened her to know that the other half of her people would never move about the village again.

Probably from sheer exhaustion and relief that others could now take over the tasks she had been doing, suddenly she felt very, very tired. When she reached her bed she lay down and slept. Sometimes she would awaken, only to fall right back to sleep again. When she finally left her bed her father's body was gone. The shelter looked tidy and clean. Members of the village had taken care of the dead. She soon learned that half of her village had died, including her father, her brother Oolark's wife and their little boy, her sister Paniagon and her husband, an aunt and her husband, as well as her uncle's wife.

After this great loss to the village, the survivors were uneasy, especially because with the death of Inerluk they had lost one of their strongest and most popular leaders. There was fear too that another such illness might suddenly strike the remaining villagers. Nedercook's older brother Nutchuk tried to quiet their fears, telling them that this had never happened before during the many generations of their people. Nevertheless, they decided to move the summer camp to a new location a little further to the west, hoping that the evil which had caused so many to die would be left behind forever. With a new summer camp the people of her village would start over again.

Nearly a year after this, with her first menstrual cycle Nedercook was considered to have become a woman by the standards of her village. Now she had to sew a piece of the softer hairless seal skin, forming a triangle with a pucker in it. This would hold the brown moss that she would use during this time. Then she had to attach it to a thin piece of leather used as a belt to tie around her waist.

4

30-30 Rifle

One day *Nedercook's older brother* Nutchuk returned from a trip up the coast. He had traded all of the items that he had taken with him to get this thing that the white man called "gun." It also had another name, "30-30 rifle," and it used what they called "shells"—all very valuable. This gun would, if you pointed it just right, kill big game much further away than one could throw a spear and it also made a big noise, like the boom of loud thunder. Nedercook made up her mind that she too would learn to use the gun.

The next winter was a hard one. The weather was often bad, and food was gone by early spring. The people fished for tomcod, but it was too early; the fish had not arrived.

Villagers went to the willows, and some ate the bark while others brought the branches home and boiled them; then they drank the liquid.

Kiachook had several pots near the little fireplace that she filled with snow for water. When anyone became too hungry, she would have them sip the hot water, then drink all that they wanted of the cold water. Villages up and down the coast were also out of food.

One day when there seemed no hope for food, an oogruk was spotted on the ice in front of the village. (Oogruk, or sea lions and seals, make holes through the sea-ice during the brighter days of spring. From these holes they crawl up onto the ice and sleep as they sun themselves.)

Everyone was whispering "Shush, shush," fearful of making a noise and scaring the mammal away. Children were cautioned to be quiet. Quickly the elders met and the best hunter was chosen to go after the oogruk. This oogruk was the hope of life for the entire village.

Nutchuk was chosen. Taking his "gun," he quietly went to the west end of the village where the willows went down a little draw. The village people quietly watched as Nutchuk made his way out to the ice. After years of stalking sleeping mammals, he knew just how short their little naps would be before they would quickly raise their heads and glance around for danger. If satisfied, the oogruk would drop its head down to nap again; if not, quicker than the blink of an eye it would slip out of sight. Each time the head lay down, Nutchuk would quickly advance. Before the head raised again, he would freeze in a crouch.

The villagers saw him sit and point his "gun" toward the oogruk. "Too far away," the old people whispered. Then everyone seemed to hold their breath. They saw the oogruk raise its head and then drop before the report of the rifle was heard. Nutchuk was up and running. As soon as he reached the oogruk, a joyful yell went up from all the onlookers. The village was saved. Life would go on. A man from the next village stopped and asked if he could have some of the meat for his people. He was not disappointed. Later the tomcod returned. People fished through holes or cracks in the ice near the shore. For another year the famine was over.

5

Copper Cave

Many years before Nedercook was born the men of her village had made some copper bracelets and other small items. The copper was supposed to have come from what they called the "Copper Cave."

A hunter who had wandered for days many miles away became lost trying to find his way home. He was traveling late, and as the dusk of evening began a fog settled over the mountains he was trying to cross over. With the poor light he was trying to descend a slope and did not notice until he started falling that he had stepped onto an incline and he began sliding and fell a few feet into a cave. It was too dark for him to see clearly, but he heard a ringing sound as he and his spear hit the bottom. In the dim light he could just make out the shape of large and small bones lying around. He tried to climb out but he always fell back to the cave floor, so he decided to wait for the morning light. He spent a fearful, sleepless night.

When the sun came up in the morning he could see that the cave went back about fifty feet and the whole interior had this strange-colored rock. Some pieces lay around so he put a few in his pack sack, one fell from his hand and he heard a sort of ringing echo sound.

There was one way that he could climb out; it was hard because the sides to the entrance were steep.

When he returned to the village the men discovered that they could make bracelets and other small pieces out of the rock. A few years later two men went with him to gather more of this strange rock.

When the men found where he had been, one almost fell in a small opening. Many rocks had fallen from the mountain above and lay all around. The opening looked so dangerous that no one wanted to go down with all the loose rocks that looked ready to fall. The next year when they returned, more of the mountainside had fallen. There was no sign of the hole, just a large pile of rock mingled with earth from the slide.

After many years the people of the village said that if one stood near Topkok looking out to sea, directly behind this person's back, many long miles away, would be the mountains from which the copper came. It was said that if a woman did not give away her copper bracelet by the time she died it would be placed in the grave with her.

The ground was often frozen when death occurred, and not having the proper tools to dig graves on frozen or thawed areas, people placed the dead on the tundra or high beaches. A tepee-like structure was placed around the body to keep dogs or other animals away. There was enough space between the poles so that if one wanted to see inside they could by getting close to the openings. This also allowed loved ones to view the departed and any treasured items that were placed with them. In time only the skeletons and the treasures could be seen.

As time passed more and more traders came along the coast with their little boats. Then came men who, when they were finished trading with the village people, walked out to the little shelters at the graves. (Early traders did not do this.) After they left, some children walked out there too, mimicking the traders, and they noticed that there were only skeletons left—the treasures were missing.

Kiachook had a beautiful carving that was passed on to her. It was so old no one could remember where it originally came from. It was old but very beautiful and highly treasured. One day three traders who came in a boat entered Kiachook's home. They were looking at the carving, passing it back and forth. Then one of the men walked around so that Kiachook had to turn her back on the other two as he asked her some unimportant questions. Then he shook her hand and said they had to leave. He hurriedly joined the two at the door and they all quickly left in their boat. Kiachook wondered for awhile where they might have placed her carving. She looked for it, but it was nowhere in her home. She never saw it again. Before this she had always trusted the traders.

As Nedercook grew older there was more and more talk of strange ships with white people coming in much larger seagoing vessels than their umiak. The white men called these "ships." It was said that some of these strange ships had something fastened above to catch the wind and the wind would then help the ship to move. Some of the ships would carry men who hunted the big bowhead whale, killing it with something that made a big noise.

6

Golovin Bay Trading Post

A *few years passed, then one day* a big ship like none they had ever seen before was visible on the horizon. They saw it anchor off from a place that would later be named Golovin Bay. They saw people similar to the traders bring boats ashore loaded with supplies. They did not know that a trading post would soon be built at this location.

Nutchuk and other men later went to see the action and hopefully make some good trades. Nutchuk returned home with a sack of white flour in a white bag. The traders said it was something good to eat. Nutchuk may have thought it was the white man's version of a seal poke full of something good. Setting it down in Kiachook's home, he carefully opened it. The bag was filled with white powdery stuff, almost the color of snow. He took a pinch to taste—it did not taste good to him. Kiachook and Nedercook each took a taste, and both said it was no good. Due to his limited understanding of the white man's language, it was not what he had expected. He took it down to the sea and dumped it into the water, saving the sack. It did not take long for the villagers to learn that the flour could be mixed with water, made

Trixie Brandon, left, wears a fancy ground squirrel-skin parka. Minnie Ferguson, right, wears a cloth covering her skin parka. Photo by Edna Wilder.

into small balls, and dropped into boiling water and cooked. At first some did not get the water hot enough at the start and it turned into a runny goo. When frying pans became available, balls of dough were cooked in hot oil.

Another day Nutchuk brought home some calico cloth for his wife and Nedercook. The two women had quite a time trying to cut this with their ulus. Both decided to make a covering for their squirrel-skin parka, which they wore with the fur side to the body. This covering would be for special occasions. Sewing this by hand was different from skin sewing. This cloth was very valuable because it took all of the biggest white ermine skins that Nutchuk had caught for several years. He had to trade fifty large skins for enough cloth to make one parka covering.

For a fifty-pound sack of flour they had to give two pairs of fancy mukluks, one tall and one of the regular length.

If the Eskimos wanted one *empty* milk can they would have to give the storekeeper one whole sealskin, cleaned and tanned by using the alder bark that turned the skin side a pretty red. They also traded for beans and potatoes. The women learned to soak dried beans overnight, boil them the next day without any seasoning, let the beans cool, then mash the beans by hand, adding cooked boiled potatoes, mixing both together until fluffy, then adding seal oil as if they were preparing Eskimo ice cream.

Women from the villages who moved to Golovin to be near the new store sewed up fur garments as fast as they could to trade for enough food for their families, because this area was not a good place for wild game. Nevertheless, Natives started moving to Golovin from up the Fish River and other places. Some of the men worked for the trading post. They learned how to build with lumber and nails; some built cabins for their families—nothing elaborate, just a square, boxlike building. They did not worry about furniture. Never having had any, they figured they did not need any. They soon learned that they had to have

Eskimo women used cloth to make covers for their squirrel-skin parkas. These parka covers were made in the 1930s and give an idea of how calico was used. By this time sewing machines were used and shared by friends. Photographer unknown.

some kind of stove and the pipe that was needed for it. Because this new kind of home was not warm and snug like their inne, on windy days the cold air would come through the cracks.

Sometime later Nedercook and her mother moved to Golovin for the summer. That same spring a young white man arrived on the first steamship from the States. George Daniels (this is not his real name) came to work for the trading post. Nedercook by now had overcome her fear of the white men and would go with her family to trade at the store. Sometimes she would go with her young friends.

Steel needles were most prized by the women for sewing the skins; next came the bright calico cloth, which could be made into outer coverings for squirrel parkas. Most of the items in the store were things Nedercook had never seen before, and, although she never asked, she would wonder what they could be used for.

George Daniels soon noticed the young Eskimo woman, and being lonely in this strange land it did not take him long to cultivate her friendship. For some reason Nedercook and her mother did not move back to the village that fall.

With the coming of winter young George was homesick and lonely. He did not like this cold, barren country where the wind blew the snow into wild blizzards. The wind would blow so strong it would form snow into hard drifts. In some places it was so hard, he did not leave a dent in it when he walked. And with all this misery, the sun hardly came above the horizon before it would quickly disappear, leaving a cold, dark world.

More and more he turned to Nedercook. Possibly, in his lonely state, he even thought that he loved her. It took a while to win her confidence, but he was handsome, and soon he was telling her that he wanted her for his wife. He explained that the white man's customs were different from hers. He said that while he was living at Golovin Bay he could not take her to live in his house. Not while he was in a foreign land. He told her often that when he took her to his mother's home, which was across the sea, she would live in his house, and they would be together forever. But for now she should stay with her mother and just come to his dwelling as his wife for an evening.

In her circle of friends, Nedercook was one of the better-looking young women. George would at times give her a box of white crackers and sometimes white flour to take home.

Nedercook fell in love. This was her first love. She believed his every word. She would go home happy and tell her mother of the different custom of the white man and of how much this man loved her.

Kiachook would listen and look at her daughter's happy face. Such a strange custom, Kiachook did not understand it. She wished that her husband Inerluk was alive. Maybe he would understand it better than she.

Nedercook, however, had no reservations. She loved young George sincerely and with all her heart.

Minnie (Nedercook). Photo by Mrs. Kenen.

One day as spring approached Nedercook knew that she was pregnant. She was overjoyed and could hardly wait to share the news with George. He had not given this much thought, but as the months passed, he noticed Nedercook's growing waistline. A little shocked, he realized that if he stayed in Alaska he would have to take the responsibility of being the father of a half-breed Eskimo child. George Daniels was not a strong man. This weighed heavily upon his mind, especially now that some missionaries had arrived and planned to build a mission or a church.

The last steamship of the season would soon be arriving at Golovin Bay. The fall days were getting darker and colder. The prospect of spending another cold, miserable winter in this windy, barren land of ice and snow . . . and then having the added responsibility of a child was too much for handsome George. *Yes*, he thought. *Wait until the day I am ready to leave and then tell her.*

Just before it would be time for Nedercook to come to his place, George went to her home. Knowing how much Nedercook loved her mother, he said that he had just received a letter from his mother and she needed him at home right away. The only way for him to go was to leave that evening on the big ship. He said he would miss her, but it was for the best if she stayed with her mother until after the baby arrived. He would come back on the first boat next spring, and then they could become a family. He was holding her as he said this, then he kissed her.

"It will be hard for me to go and leave you. . . . You can make it easier for me by not coming down to the dock to say goodbye, just kiss me now. . . . Promise?"

This was all so sudden and unexpected. Nedercook was not prepared for it, but she promised that she would try to help him by not coming down to the dock to see him off. She loved him and would do anything to help him.

Darkness falls quickly in September. Under this cover Nedercook could not resist walking to a pile of driftwood, stacked tepee fashion on the beaches so that it could be found and harvested after the snows of winter. Standing hidden next to this, she had a good view of the dock, which was fairly well lit. It was nearly time for the passengers to leave. It hurt Nedercook to see George looking so happy and to hear his laughter faintly carried over the sound of the tugboat's engines as it stood by, ready to move the barge as soon as it was loaded with passengers and baggage. As the passengers stepped away from the light he was soon lost in the darkness. All she could see was a dark mass on the dark form of the barge. She watched until the tugboat's light reached the steamship. Returning home, she sobbed in her mother's arms.

That same fall Nedercook and her mother moved back to their inne at the village, knowing that it would be less drafty and cold for the baby's birth. Nedercook kept active. She walked, hunted, sewed up fur items for sale, and fished for tomcod. It comforted her a little to think that George looked happy when he was leaving because he was going to see his mother. She missed him very much.

On New Year's Day she had a baby boy. Kiachook was a great help. Having the baby made Nedercook feel closer to George. It was hard for her to wait for spring and the arrival of the first boat. She made the prettiest little mukluks and parka for the baby. She wanted him to look good when George saw him for the first time. She made sure that she and her mother returned to their little cabin at Golovin Bay long before it was time for the first steamboat's arrival.

The day the first boat docked at Golovin Bay, Nedercook could hardly contain herself. She and the baby, named J.D., waited eagerly a short ways off from the group that had gathered to meet the passengers.

Nedercook's heart was beating fast as she checked the passengers. George was not with the first barge. She wondered what had happened to him. He had promised to come back on the first steamboat. Much later, when she was certain he was not on the ship, she carried little J.D. back to Kiachook's comforting arms.

Next day her girlfriend stopped by with a letter addressed to her. Nedercook's excitement was evident as she opened the envelope that contained a sheet of paper with some handwriting and a ten-dollar bill. Her friend could not read, neither could Nedercook, so they walked to the mission. The message said, "Dear Nedercook, Hope you are well. Mother still needs me." It was signed simply "George." There was no mention of little J.D. or the money. Nedercook was disappointed. Then she thought, *Maybe he did not have time to write more.* With that consolation, she tucked his letter in her pocket.

The summer passed quickly. She sewed for cash, picked berries, and did the usual things she had learned to do. But she made sure to be at the dock with little J.D. every time the steamboat arrived. Each time she was disappointed...but she reasoned he was waiting for the last trip of the steamship. Making sure to be there in time she watched the passengers arrive. Again she was disappointed, but somehow this was worse because it was the last chance before freeze-up.

Her friend came a little later with a letter for her. She was filled with joy. When she opened it, there was a five-dollar bill and a small sheet with his handwriting. Desperate to know what he said, she hurried to the mission. The woman, a kindly person, read it to her: "Dear Nedercook, Here is some money. Do not wait for me. I am not ever coming back to Alaska, George." Like the first letter, there was no return address and no last name.

"He is not coming back?" Nedercook asked.

"He is not coming back...ever," the lady said in a sad but kindly voice.

If written words could break a heart, they broke Nedercook's. Because he had made a promise, she could not understand why he was not coming back. As before there was no mention of their baby. Had he forgotten?...No.

Feeling as if her whole world was going to pieces, Nedercook started walking out of the little settlement. She walked not caring or even noticing where she went. She just wanted to leave behind the ache in her heart. Finally she stopped and sat on a little moundlike part of the tundra, the words "I am not coming back...ever" going over and over in her mind. She put her hands to her face, trembling as the tears began to run down her face and hands. She began to sob silently, then without being aware, she was crying loudly.

Above her wails she became aware of the cries of her baby. She had forgotten that he was sleeping in her parka on her shoulders. Ashamed, she quickly slipped him into her arms, wiping her face with her hand. She began to talk soft, comforting words as she breast-fed him. She felt better. If George was not coming back she had little J.D. to take care of, and she had her mother, who she knew loved her.

7

Evil Songs

The people who came on the big ship had built a mission building and church services were held on Sundays. They canvassed the little settlement of natives, imploring them to come to church. Soon the mission found an Eskimo man who knew some English. He stood near the preacher and translated his words as closely as he understood them. It is possible that the translation of the preacher's sermon made it sound harsher than intended. He said that if they did not believe and become Christians, when they died, their spirits would go to a place called hell. Hell was a place that was very hot, and once they got there they would not be able to leave. He also said that the preacher wanted to warn them that pretty soon the world would be coming to an end. Then anyone who was still alive would have a terrible time. Women who tried to breast-feed their hungry, crying babies would have no milk in their breasts, because there would be no food, and there would be no water at all...only pools of blood on the ground. This was why it was so important that they attend the church and be saved before this bad time came. This was very frightening to Nedercook and the natives. Nedercook never forgot what the translator told them on this Sunday.

The missionaries believed that the poor Eskimos should be baptized as soon as possible. When the translation was over, Nedercook, who had come with the others, sat in fear. The preacher then walked down the aisles with a container. He sprinkled a little water on Nedercook's forehead, and mumbled something that she did not understand and said, "Hereafter you shall be known as Minnie." Moving on he sprinkled other foreheads from the container as he gave each a name. Nedercook, like many of the attending Eskimos, did not fully understand the meaning of this ritual.

The missionaries figured that the church needed a choir. With the help of the translator they worked to translate the hymns into symbols that the singers would understand. They could not read music, but they could follow a tune once they heard it sung in the English language. Soon they were singing hymns in both languages. After the natives learned to sing the hymns, the preacher forbade the Eskimos to sing any of their own native songs. The preacher told them not to ever sing their own traditional songs again, because their songs were the songs of the devil. And the devil was an evil spirit that was trying to get their soul. The preacher came down hard on this, having the interpreter tell them that when they died they would go to hell. And hell was where the devil lived, and that any Eskimo who continued to sing their native songs would surely go there when they died. And they would burn forever because they would never be able to leave.

Nedercook decided she liked the old songs, and she was sure that they were not the songs of the devil, whoever he was. Because as far back as her people could remember these were the songs they had sung, and the devil had not come after them. So when she wanted to sing the songs that she had learned so carefully as a child, she would go out on the tundra until she was sure that no one could hear her, especially the missionaries. There she would sing, sometimes singing all the songs that she had learned as a child.

A short time after this the missionaries decided to teach the Eskimos how to read English. They set up class on certain days. Many natives from up the river and others attended. Nedercook refused to attend the class, because she did not like the way they had forbidden her and her people to sing the songs that she loved. Many years later she regretted having passed up this opportunity.

Like most of the Eskimos of her time, during her early years she did a small amount of smoking and occasionally chewed some plug tobacco. The missionaries preached against this too. This did not make an impression on Nedercook because she was still upset about the ban on singing her beloved songs. She could not bring herself to believe that the songs were evil. Years later when she moved away from Golovin she continued to sing her beloved songs without fear.

8

White Crackers for Lost Love

When the next summer passed and George Daniels had not returned, Nedercook and her mother moved back to their inne at the village of Rocky Point. She continued to sew, hunt, and learned to shoot Nutchuk's "gun," which was exciting, but her heart still longed for her boy's father. White man's flour reminded her of the small sacks George would give to her along with the white hard crackers or biscuits. To ease the memories she still carried for this lost love, she and her dearest friend decided that they would eat mostly the white flour either cooked in oil or boiled, and to this diet they added the hard white crackers. This practice may not have been the best, but at the time they thought it was a fine idea.

With the passing of time they both became weak, and eventually they both became bedridden. Neither one could get up and walk. Both felt helpless. Kiachook did most of the caring for little J.D., who was now walking and quite active. No one knew what was wrong with the two women. The villagers had always considered these two to be the strongest, most active, and talented of their young women. Now both lay helpless. Word of the two women's condition soon traveled up and down the coast.

9

Arthur Samuel Tucker

Arthur Samuel Tucker, born in Norwich, Norfolk, England, was a well-educated young man who was taught to be a gentleman and to practice the reserve and refinement of his people. He enjoyed reading. Since childhood he had read everything about America that he could.

Whenever his uncle, who was a successful medical doctor in Montana, wrote to his family, Sam would have his daydreams of that faraway land. With his dreams came the longing to see in person this land where his uncle lived.

One day his uncle thought how jolly it would be to have his nephew come for a visit. He was delighted when his offer was accepted.

The trip across the sea was a new and exciting experience. Montana was everything that he had imagined and more. His uncle took him around, showing him as much as he could. When his uncle was busy Sam would be on his own. The American way of life, so free of the standard formality he had always known, appealed to Sam. Life was great in America, and so was his uncle. As Sam's visit neared the end, he was thinking of excuses he might use to stay longer. Then, overnight it seemed, the newspapers were filled with articles, stories, and black-and-white photos of the gold miners who had returned from Alaska and the Yukon Territory. Pictures showed miners with pokes full of gold, some with large nuggets. Suddenly gold fever seemed everywhere. There were pictures of steamships leaving the port of Seattle, loaded to capacity with men and equipment, off to make their fortune in the frozen North.

Sam was swept up in the excitement and wanted to go North to get in on the gold rush before all the gold was taken from the ground. He did not know much about gold mining, but from the stories in the papers it did not seem too hard.

He persuaded his uncle to let him join in the rush and together they traveled to Seattle. With his uncle's help, Sam found what he thought would be needed to survive for a good year in the North. His uncle hated to see him leave, but still he supported the trip, remembering his own departure from the motherland as a young man. In fact, if it had not been for his uncle's influence, Sam would not have been able to leave on the next steamship, the captain claiming no vacancy.

Parting gifts from his uncle, besides cash, were two medical books on illness, injury, and the treatment of such.

"Sam," his uncle said, "regardless of anything, keep these books with you at all times. Don't ever give them up, because you are going to a wild, untamed country. One day they may save your life."

As the overcrowded steamer left, the doctor watched with some misgiving and a little envy, knowing that if he were younger he too would be on that ship. The trip North was a rough one until they reached the Inside Passage. Sam thought this was a wonderful, beautiful country with the calm waters and the abundant sea life. He would stay up late, but he also loved to see the early morning fog that made things hazy. Everyone was excited when the town of Skagway came into view.

The passengers and equipment were not allowed to go ashore there, however. They were hurriedly put ashore a little further on, at Dyea. Sam, who had been trying to lose his English accent and talk more like the Americans, thought that he had succeeded quite well. As he was checking ashore the man in charge asked, "How long have you been over here from England?"

Once ashore everything seemed like bedlam to Sam. Some of the stampeders were so anxious to be the first ashore that shouting and pushing got rough. The captain soon called a halt, saying that anyone who did not behave would be taken back to the port of Seattle. He also gave orders for everyone to stay a good distance back and not come forward until all the equipment and baggage were unloaded—then wait for his order to do so. There were piles and piles of supplies and equipment, all unloaded haphazardly in a hurry, until everything brought North was put on Alaska soil.

Standing by the ship's deck were three men who back in those days might be dubbed "city dudes," dressed in light city clothes with top hats. The cold wind blowing down from the snow-covered mountains was enough to convince them to stay aboard the ship and return with it.

On this cold, snow-covered land, Sam had to find and then carry his wall tent (in those days the material was heavy) to a place away from the others and locate the rest of his supplies: Yukon stove, containers of food, sleeping bag, warm clothes and boots, gold pan, pick, shovel, and axe—there seemed no end.

To Sam the whole atmosphere held an urgency bordering on madness as the men rushed around collecting their belongings. Everyone wanted to be the first to reach Dawson City and get in on the gold strike before it was too late. Sam pitched his tent away from the others, then he gathered the rest of his belongings, carrying everything to his tent. Determination can work wonders, and by evening Sam had set up his tent, placed his belongings and food inside, built a fire in the little stove, cooked, and ate.

Thus began the first of many tired nights he would spend alone. As he drifted off to sleep he wondered what his family would think if they could see him now.

Men climbing Chilkoot Pass, c. 1897. Courtesy Alaska State Library, Early Prints of Alaska Photograph Collection, image no. P297-216.

The next day the hardest part of his trip was just beginning. All of his belongings had to be moved from his tent to near the base of the back-breaking incline called the Chilkoot Pass.

It would take many days and much labor. Some things were carried on the back, but one could only carry so much. Sleds loaded and necked (pulled by a rope that went over the shoulder next to the neck) were used to slowly haul a load to the base of the steep incline. If one had the strength, this worked better than a single pack, but it was hard and exhausting labor. From there it was harder still to carry one's belongings up the steep incline to the summit. Once the summit was reached each person piled his load a little way off from the trail and put his name visibly on top. Surprisingly, no one bothered or took anyone else's belongings. Perhaps the shared experience of the hard work involved gave each a feeling of respect for another's property, because everyone's goal was to reach Dawson City.

For some, all this was too much. They just gave up and returned to the boat landing, selling their belongings for a ticket back home. Some of the stampeders hired dog teams to help get their belongings to the base of the summit. Horses were also used, but many of the overworked animals died along the trail.

Sam was able to buy a small sled from one of the men going back to the States. Each day he struggled with his loads. At night he would practically fall into his bed. Eventually he got all of his belongings to the top. Getting them down the other side on the sled was not the easy trip he thought it would be; often it was steep and slippery. Finally he had his tent set up at the bottom. On the last trip down the joy he felt to finally be over the mountain made him less cautious. He slipped, and tumbled down to the bottom of the incline. His hurts and bruises were many. He felt great pain in his right shoulder. After gathering his scattered supplies he managed to make it to his tent. From the books his uncle had given to him he figured he had dislocated his shoulder. The remedy did not seem hard. The arm had to be pulled out and given a twist to get it back in place. This was not possible to do alone. One man stopped long enough to help him. The man pulled and twisted on Sam's arm and nothing happened but more pain. Next day two men tried to pull and twist his arm, but like the day before it only caused him more pain and suffering. He asked the men who passed by to please send a doctor his way if they happened to meet one.

Sam hated to have the days go by while he was more or less stuck at his tent, but he had no choice. On the third day a man came to his tent and asked if he was the man with the shoulder trouble. Sam removed his shirt and was prepared for another session of pain from the yanking and twisting that was sure to come. The stranger first carefully examined Sam's arm and shoulder, then with gentle hands he felt around, pushing his finger here and there and asking if it hurt. The man made a quick movement and Sam felt his shoulder slip back in place. He could hardly believe how effortlessly the man had done it. The stranger proved to be a medical doctor who had always wanted to see Alaska and the Yukon Territory. It was with relief and joy that Sam offered to pay him whatever he asked. "No, it was nothing," the doctor said, smiling and refusing any payment.

Breakup was starting, making travel by day too tough with the soft, slushy snow and ice. Sam would travel after the evening temperatures cooled and froze the soft snow until the sun rose next morning. It took a lot of hard work but eventually he made it to Lake Bennett. The men who had so hurriedly passed him were camped by its shore. Breakup comes fast in the North, making the lake ice too rotten for travel. One man who had some dogs felt that he could not be delayed waiting for the ice to completely melt and go out of the lake. He loaded his sled with his belongings, hitched up his dogs, and took off, only to break through the ice a short distance from shore. Soaking wet, along with his belongings, he was rescued by those he had planned to leave behind.

The only way to go on now was to build a boat and wait for the ice to go out, then sail or paddle on. Boats of many kinds and shapes were being built from any material that was available.

Trees were cut, limbed, and sawed into lumber by hand, usually by two men, one on each end of a long saw. Any available scrap material was used.

When Sam pulled into camp, some of the men he had become acquainted with asked if he would help them to build a boat. In exchange he could put his belongings on it and ride with them to Dawson. Sam agreed and pitched his tent beside theirs.

With the warmer weather the mosquitoes came out and were quite a nuisance to everyone. Sam marveled at how quickly after breakup ducks, geese, swans, cranes, and songbirds arrived, all heading north while so much snow was still on shaded areas and riverbeds.

When they finished their boat, it was not the best-looking one, but they hoped that it would hold water and, most important, carry the men and their belongings.

Finally the lake was free of ice. It looked safe to launch the boats—the ride to Dawson was on!

Boats of all kinds and sizes left the shore of Lake Bennett. The stampeders' hopes rose again.

Getting around the dangerous rapids was hard work, but eventually they arrived at Dawson City, Yukon Territory. Dawson City was not a place where gold was lying around to be picked up. Sam and his friends had to find un-staked land and then dig the shafts by pick and shovel to find gold... if they were lucky. They came close a few times, but the gold was on two adjoining claims. They dug the shafts and panned samples as they progressed, but all they ever found were a few colors. The gold on their claims was much too scarce for a pick-and-shovel operation. They spent the days of spring digging and panning, like hundreds of other men who did not make a gold strike.

When the month of July arrived, the miners were all many miles away from their homes and felt the need to celebrate a day that they were familiar with—the Fourth of July!

From the surrounding hills they came to Dawson City. The streets of Dawson became alive with lonely men, coming and going to the bars. Some stayed out on the streets, and because they missed the sound of firecrackers, shot their pistols or other guns into the sky or the river. There was so much racket and noise going on that all the loose dogs, and those that could break loose, took off in fear, swimming across the Yukon River to safety on the other side.

Sam would recall this as one of the wildest Fourth of Julys that he had ever experienced.

Digging through the summer months proved to be just more hard work with only a few colors at times. Good strikes in other areas kept their hopes up. With the coming of winter the temperature dropped, at times reaching forty below zero and colder.

With the arrival of snow and cold weather Sam's friends decided a cabin would be better than tents. With Sam's help they built a small cabin, but Sam decided to spend the winter in his tent. When the men did not have the time to go to the river with containers for water they would melt snow. Sam's upbringing included a bath on Saturday evenings. For this he melted snow in his gold pan by placing it on the little Yukon stove. He would take a sponge bath, even when the temperature outside of his tent was forty or more below zero.

News has a way of traveling, and news of a gold strike at Nome, Alaska, came during the cold of winter. Again, miners got the gold fever. Stories told of gold lying on the beach at Nome and in the nearby hills. How to get there before it was all gone filled the thoughts of the lucky and the unlucky prospectors.

Many decided to build boats and go down the Yukon River after breakup. Sam and his friends were no different. But they did not have the materials to build a boat, as wood by now was a scarce commodity. They decided to build a raft by using whatever would keep them above water and float down the river, and then find a way to St. Michaels and from there to Nome by small boat. They spent the rest of the winter building the raft.

Floating down the Yukon River on the raft was one of Sam's truly peaceful experiences, to be remembered for the rest of his life. On other days, when snags, sandbars, rocks, and sweepers were of imminent danger, everyone was too busy trying to guide the raft safely by these dangers to enjoy the beauty.

Toward evening they would pull to shore and make camp for the night, cooking their meals over a campfire. Sitting around it, they reminisced and laughed, telling tales of their pasts while the fire burned low. They spread their bedding beneath the large spruce trees, and as they drifted off to sleep they would listen to the songs or chirps of birds that mingled with the sounds of the mighty river.

Sometimes they would camp at the confluence of a clear little stream, catching fresh fish for dinner. Sam loved falling asleep to the sounds of the small babbling streams.

After making a trade for their raft and some equipment they got a small boat to take them to St. Michaels. From there they got passage on a larger boat that was leaving for Nome. As they neared the town of Nome they could see the white tents placed all over the beach and on the surrounding tundra and hillsides. *Looks like another disappointment*, Sam thought, and he was right. They were put to shore and found there were no open places to camp. Those who had come before had claimed sections of the beach and did not want any strangers moving in. It was the same on the tundra. You had to have a claim in order to camp because the prospectors were everywhere.

The beach held every kind of rig for panning or rocking out gold, many of which Sam had never seen before. Sam and his friends finally found a place out of town where they could camp, and although they tried to find good gold-bearing ground, they could not. To survive each had to go their separate way to find work.

The weather had been very rainy ever since they arrived in Nome. After a couple of weeks of steady rain Sam asked an Eskimo man, "Does it rain here like this all the time?"

"No, no," said the man, "pretty soon snow!"

Sam did odd jobs to take him through the winter while still trying to save money. Wondering how Nome got its name, he was told that the early map makers had asked an old resident of the area, "Do you know what this place is called?"

He replied with, "Naumee," or a similar sound that meant "no" in his Eskimo language. So the map maker, trying to figure out how to spell that strange-sounding name, came up with the spelling of Nome.

10

Bluff City

Another gold strike filled the news. It was reported that gold was so plentiful at Bluff City that young Eskimo children were playing with it on the beach, letting the sun glint and shine on the pretty golden sand as it sifted down from their hands. Sam had a week to finish the job he had promised to do before he could join the stampede. When he finished there was no transportation left because by then much of the town had departed, taking all that was available. Sam had worked and walked so much since leaving England, he decided that rather than wait an unknown time for transportation he would walk the sixty-five miles or more to Bluff City. He packed his belongings and left them with the man he had worked for and asked him to ship them on the next available way to the new goldfield. With only a medium pack he made the trip in three days, stopping here and there at interesting places.

As he came in sight of Bluff City he knew it would be another disappointment. It was a repeat of Dawson City and Nome. Tents were everywhere, even on the beach. It was a wild tent city. Fighting broke out over a mining-claim dispute. After still more fighting a man was killed. Word was sent to Nome and a dozen military men arrived. During this period every woman, white or native, was ordered to stay in her home until law and order of a kind was once again restored.

Sam liked this part of Alaska. It was barren but he still liked it. He decided to find work with anyone who could pay for his time while he became more familiar with the area. He got permission from the mining company he worked for to build a cabin on the hillside overlooking the little town. He would spend his off hours gathering logs from the beaches. Each storm usually brought more. There were a lot of dry logs on the other beaches besides the one in front of the little town. Sam kept busy during the evenings and on his days off completing his log cabin before winter.

Sam needed a stove for his cabin but it was too late to order one, because with freezing nights the shipping season was over. Sam talked to the company blacksmith and had him make a big stove with an extra-large door so that Sam would be able to burn stumps and driftwood without spending a lot of time sawing wood by hand. When he had a fire in it, he could use it as a cookstove to boil or fry food. Sometimes when the fire was not too hot he even made toast by placing the slices on top of the stove and turning them over when they browned. If the stove was very hot he placed them in a frying pan to toast.

11

Billy G.

Sam made several friends, one we will call Billy G. During this time there were very few white women living in this little settlement. One was a pretty married woman. She and Billy G. got into a situation that appeared to be more than casual friends. Her husband became jealous and he sent word to Nome, asking for a marshal to come to Bluff City and arrest this troublemaker, Billy G. As in most small settlements word got around fast, and Billy G. soon learned that a marshal was in town looking for him. Scared and not knowing what to do, he came knocking on Sam's door.

"Sam," he said in despair, "help me.... Because the marshal is looking for me. Right now he is searching every house in town."

Sam looked out from his window, which overlooked the small town. He saw the marshal emerge from a building, looking around. He had searched everywhere except the little cabin on the hillside. He started toward the cabin.

"See, he is coming! Sam—please help me," young Billy G. said in despair. Sam looked around his room. "If I help you, will you do exactly as I tell you?"

"I will do anything," begged Billy G.

"OK," said Sam as he opened the big square door on the stove the blacksmith had made. "I've not had a fire in it for days. Get in, but *keep quiet* when he comes. Remember, any noise and he will find you!"

Sam took a seat by the table, and continued with a letter that he was writing to his sister Maude, in England. Soon there was a loud knock on the door. Sam walked over and opened it. The marshal introduced himself and Sam did too. Then the marshal asked if he lived alone.

"Yes," replied Sam.

"I am looking for a man named Billy G.," said the marshall. "Mind if I look around?"

"Help yourself," Sam said, as he walked back to where he had laid his pen down. Picking it up he wiped the nib before the ink dried, placing it beside the partly written letter.

The marshal looked under the bed—nothing! With a sudden move he threw back the bed covers—nothing! He looked around the room; there was just no other place for a man to hide.

"Well, I have a long trip back to Nome so I've got to hurry," the marshal said as he headed for the door. Turning he continued, "The man must have skipped town, for I have looked in every house. Sorry to have bothered you."

Sam watched in silence as the marshal walked swiftly back to the roadhouse.

"OK, you can come out now," Sam said as he opened the stove door. With a bit of a struggle, a disheveled, dusty, soot-blackened Billy G. emerged smiling from ear to ear.

"You had better wait until the marshal leaves town before you go outside to dust off—so have a chair," Sam said. Soon after this, the jealous man took his wife and left town with no plans to return.

12

First Alaskan Hunt

Sam *was up before daylight* on this brisk December morning. Later he looked out the window, and by the early light he could see new snow that had fallen during the night, making everything clean and white.

He had not had any fresh meat for a long time, but was living on dried beans and ham with a sprinkling of dried onions boiled together—if lucky, a can of tomatoes or some ketchup was added and a good sprinkling of pepper.

He had never hunted with a rifle, but he owned one and thought this would be a good day to try for one of the large arctic hares. These rabbits were ten to twelve pounds in weight. He had eaten some at a friend's place and they had tasted so good.

Taking his rifle, a box of shells, and an empty pack sack, he went back across the tundra until he reached the end of the cliffs. This little creek was called Kiana Creek and was about two miles long. At the mouth of the creek on the west side there was a cliff that went up the creek for about three or four hundred feet, where it tapered to an end, where dog teams or people on foot could follow the creek back down to the beach in front of Sam's cabin. From there the cliff continued around this beach and then along the coast west to Bluff City. Going up the creek he could follow along on one side of the willows that grew thickly on each side of this creek. Sam could see fresh rabbit tracks in the new snow, and he thought that this was exciting. After going for about a mile and not seeing a rabbit he decided to walk back toward the mouth of the creek. From this point the creek would drop considerably until it reached the cliffs in front of his cabin.

The incline was even steeper where the water dropped as it flowed to the sea. Now of course it was frozen slick and smooth. When Sam was where the creek first began to drop at the beginning of the cliffs, he thought he saw a rabbit. He shifted the rifle to his left hand as he quickly jacked a shell into the rifle. Excited, he continued walking to get a better view of the rabbit, which was hidden partly by the willows. He thought he had better get ready to shoot in case it started to run, so he cocked the rifle. Expecting to shoot any minute , he looked more closely and saw it was only a snow-covered mound about the size of a rabbit.

Disappointed, Sam continued to walk down the creek in front of the cliffs. There were fresh rabbit tracks all around as he continued on. He was looking around for rabbits and not paying any attention to what was underfoot. Suddenly he began to slip and slide on the slick, snow-covered ice. He started to fall and as he did, his right hand went up and out. Somehow he must have touched or put pressure on the trigger of the cocked gun, because it went off as he hit hard on the ice. He heard the gun go off, and it felt as if something had touched his right hand.

When he stood up he looked down at his right mitten and saw a hole going through it. He felt no pain, but he was scared because he was not sure what he would see when he pulled his mitten off. When the mitten was off he saw, to his horror, that the bullet had hit his first two fingers, breaking both bones. They were white and bloodless. Sam felt faint, but before he could move his hand, he felt the pain coming and suddenly everything turned red. Blood began to gush and drip from his hand. He knew he must get to his cabin quickly before losing too much blood. This was beyond his care.

Knowing he must get to a doctor as soon as possible, he hurried as best he could. While carrying the rifle with his left hand, he retraced his steps back up the creekbed until the cliffs ended. From there he could get to the top of the tundra and to his cabin. He hurriedly bandaged his hand to stop the flow of blood. He could not go the eighty miles or so to the doctor in Nome by himself. (This was before any telephone communication was available.) Sam did not know what to do; he felt helpless.

Desperately he hoped that one of his Eskimo friends from the little village of Chiukak would come by—if not him, then anybody. He paced about in the cabin. The pain was worse. He stood by the window hoping to see a dog team, any dog team. Then he saw a team coming west on the trail that dog teams were using since the sea-ice had frozen over.

As it drew near he tried to signal. The ever-alert Eskimo—who turned out to be Sam's friend Tim—saw him and turned his team to the mouth of the creek, then up onto the tundra to the cabin. Sam explained the urgency of making the trip to Nome as soon as possible. He would pay the man to take him.

It was a painful disappointment when Tim said he could not take him that day. He had a family, and they would worry. He also had to go back to the village for more and better dogs. He would borrow some of the faster ones—enough to pull two men—because it would take them at least two hard days of driving from his village to Nome. Dry fish would also be needed to feed his dogs for the trip there and back. He would leave very early the next morning and be at Sam's cabin by daybreak. Sam thanked Tim . . . he was his only hope.

Sam collected what he thought he would need for the trip. There would be no way to heat the cabin while he was away, so he emptied the containers of water because when they froze the expansion would damage the containers. Then there was nothing much he could do but wait out the pain-filled hours until Tim returned. At the break of day Tim arrived with eleven strong dogs. He had also brought a fur robe, which he placed next to the back of the sled, then he motioned for Sam to get onto it. When Sam was on the fur robe, Tim tucked it carefully around him and they were off.

This was a lonely, barren part of the rough trail they traveled. With no trees for shelter the wind had no mercy as it increased, blowing drifting snow as the team rushed on. Sam was thankful for Tim's foresight in bringing the fur robe, because sitting still in the sled would have dangerously chilled him. The trip seemed to become endless by the time they saw the lights of the Solomon Roadhouse. The dogs were getting tired. It was dark, so they spent the night.

The hot food was so comforting and both were treated very well. The owner's wife tried her best to help Sam with his bandaged hand, promising to wake them before daybreak for breakfast. They left in the early dawn. Tim was good at driving the team, and though they had many fast turns he managed not to let the sled tip over. Sam suffered in silence through the day. There seemed no end to the trail and Sam was wondering how much longer he would be able to stand the pain when, turning a point in the road, the first lights of Nome could be seen far ahead.

"I am going to make it after all," Sam sighed.

Seeing the lights helped to keep Sam's hope up as they neared the little town of Nome. When they were beginning to pass the first cabins at the edge of town, a dog team coming from the opposite direction brought a wild rush to Tim's dogs. Tim's dogs were not used to the smell of strange dogs from another place, and instead of passing they began barking and made a wild rush straight for the oncoming dog team. Soon both teams were in a death-or-survival fight. Sam was surprised by this wild behavior, because he was under the impression that

Tim had been pushing these dogs to near exhaustion. To see them all erupt in this wild fighting frenzy was a shock.

A stranger who came to help stop the fighting and to separate the teams was viciously bitten and had to leave. Tim and the man driving the other team had to use their whips to stop the fight. After the other team was on its way, Sam suggested to Tim that it might be wise to give up driving into town and just find a secluded place where the dogs could be tied, with less danger of someone, especially a child, being bitten.

Sam and Tim set out on foot to find the doctor. When they finally did, the pain was hard for Sam to bear. The doctor seemed like a kindly person. He examined Sam's hand, then asked, "When did this happen?" Then he continued, "I will have to operate, but the light is too bad now. Come back before noon tomorrow and we will do it by best daylight." Seeing the disappointment in Sam's face and knowing the pain he must be suffering, the doctor gave him something to relieve the pain and some pain pills to take with him until the next day.

The next day, after the operation as he finished bandaging Sam's hand, the doctor said, "I put your fingers in a glass of preservative. It is on the windowsill. Would you like to take them with you when you go home?"

"No, thank you," Sam said, remembering all the pain they had caused him.

The doctor asked Sam to stay in town for a little over a week so he could check the healing.

The doctor did a fine job. Everything healed properly without ugly scars and, unlike some operations, without pain at the point where the fingers were removed. Sam could touch anything without feeling pain from the nerve endings in the end of his fingers.

Tim was a big help starting a fire in Sam's stove and getting the house warm again before he left. During the following days and weeks he cut and split wood, made trips to Bluff City to get mail and supplies, and helped Sam with anything that he could. He asked nothing in return. Sam did not forget his kindness, and later he did some good things for Tim and his family.

After Sam's hand had completely healed, being minus the two fingers did not stop him from doing whatever he wanted to do. As the years passed, Sam became known in that area as "Ugh-ga-tork" or "As-ga-tork." This word in the Eskimo language means "missing fingers." So he became known as "the man with missing fingers."

13

We Are Going to Be Lost

Late one afternoon Sam was returning home after visiting with his friends who lived at the little village of Chiukak, located a little over twelve miles to the east. Sam had put together a small team of dogs, making sure that each dog was friendly and non-biting. One, a large, powerful, intelligent dog, showed great promise, and Sam trained this one to be his lead dog. He took good care of his dogs and they responded well to his commands.

These last few weeks of cold November weather had frozen the ice for more than two miles out from shore. To make travel easier for his dogs Sam decided to take the newly made trail that the first traveler had picked on the frozen Bering Sea ice rather than the trail over the uneven hills and gullies, which would be longer and harder. (After freeze-up often a strong storm would come from a southerly direction. Old-timers called these storms a "sou'wester." High winds coming from the open water pressured the ice until it cracked, forming rough piles of broken ice along the break. Some would be small but others left huge chunks standing in all angles, especially if the ice was thick.)

On the trail, a short distance in front of Sam, an Eskimo man was also traveling west with his dog team. Both teams traveled at a good speed. As Sam stood on the sled runners this quiet evening, holding onto the handlebars, his mind was lost in thought. He did not notice the strange stillness that filled the air. Sam had not lived in this area long and many things were still new to him.

Suddenly the man ahead called his dogs to halt. Sam stopped his. The man ahead was pointing toward the shore. Sam saw a thin dark line and knew instantly what it meant—the Bering Sea ice that they were traveling on had broken away from the shore ice and was drifting out to sea. There was no wind, just this strange stillness. Both teams turned and drove as fast as they could toward shore and the open water. As they drew nearer, Sam's heart sank with fear because the width of the water could be seen in proper perspective. It was wide—too wide—almost a quarter of a mile by the time they reached the edge. Both men stood looking at the dark, cold water, which seemed to widen each minute.

"We are going to be lost," the Eskimo man said sadly.

Sam had heard many times of how dangerous it was to travel on the Bering Sea ice and of those who had been taken out to sea in winter, just as it was now taking him and his companion. There was nothing they could do. The water was freezing cold. A person would not last but a few minutes, even if he was a good swimmer. Of all the people that had been taken out to sea on ice like this, none had ever returned. Now it was taking him and his companion. This was very frightening.

"What can we do?" Sam knew it was useless to ask but he had to ask anyway.

"I don't know, nothing I guess." Then the man continued in a voice of utter despair, "Nobody ever live that I know of who go out on ice like this."

They both felt like hollering for help, but there was no one to hear them.

"Let's go on," suggested Sam. "Maybe someone at Bluff City will see us and come out in a kayak." (In this time period a kayak would be their only means of help.)

Without further word each turned their teams to the west. Darkness was falling as they traveled on. There was a strange quiet stillness in the air that even Sam was now aware of. Soon there came a gentle swirling breeze. Then the north wind struck with a fury. Even in the diminishing light they could see the whitecaps being blown in the water toward the ice. After what seemed like hours they saw the few glimmering lights of Bluff City. They saw also what looked like a bonfire on the snow-covered beach. As they watched they noticed that the waves from the strong wind were breaking chunks of ice from the edge in front of them. Both knew that as they drifted further out to sea the piece of ice they were on would slowly break to pieces. By now the wind was throwing sprays of cold water onto them and the dogs, driving a chill through their bodies. As they watched the lights of the little town grow dimmer, a terrible feeling of loneliness and despair filled their hearts.

"We can't do anything here, so let's go further west while we can," suggested Sam. "Maybe the ice we are on will get closer to shore as we pass Cape Nome and somebody will come in a kayak and get us." What they did not know was that the Eskimos were aware that two people had been taken out on the ice. A traveler on the hilly trail had seen two teams, but they were too far away to identify. Men had rushed to the edge of the water with their kayaks, but the wind was so strong they knew that it was useless to try. In despair they had built the fire on the beach.

Sam figured that the ice had broken loose down toward Rocky Point and now was traveling west toward Cape Nome. Beyond there it was all water. Away from land the wind would make the waves bigger and the ice would soon break to pieces.

Sam hoped and prayed with all the deep, trusting faith that his mother had taught him back at their home in England, which now seemed so very far away.

Traveling was hard. Darkness soon made traveling over the rough ice too dangerous. Coming to a stop, they could feel the movement of the ice below their feet. The dogs sensed this too and became uneasy. Sam decided it was best to move back and get away from the salty spray. They watched as the relentless wind and waves tore at the ice, breaking off pieces and chunks.

"We have to stop now because it is getting too dark," Sam said. "I think we should get away from this edge before it falls apart. Let's go to solid ice further out." Keeping close to each other, they moved back past the wet spray to where it might be safe for the night. They stopped the teams and made sure that the dogs would be secure and not get away during the night. "We have to stay here tonight," Sam said to his friend then asked, "Can you build a snow shelter so we can get out of this wind?" They built a crude shelter from some pieces of loose ice from a pressure ridge, and cut hard snow with the long-bladed wooden knife that his friend carried strapped to the sled for this purpose in case he was ever caught out on the tundra. With no moon this was a hard task, but they finished a shelter before the night became pitch-black. The lights of Bluff City were out of sight. Sam dreaded what might happen if they both crawled into the shelter and fell asleep. He decided that one team, with the back of the sled, should be secured at the shelter, then the other sled tied to the front of the first team so it could be freed in a hurry if necessary. He suggested that they each take turns resting while the other carefully followed along beside the dogs and the tow line to the end of the last team, and back again. Doing this in the dark for a few times took a long time, but it gave the one in the shelter a welcome respite from the cruel north wind.

To Sam this night felt like the longest of his life. Hope was hard to keep in his heart, but he tried, and he silently prayed as he groped his way along from dog to dog in the dark. Far away it seemed there was another flickering light. When he finished his turn he called to his friend and they both looked longingly at the dim light.

"Friends build a fire for us," commented his companion.

"Where do you think it is?" Sam asked.

"Maybe Solomon or Cape Nome, too dark to be sure," was the reply.

After a night that seemed like it would never end, a faint light began to show toward the east. Sam made it back to the snow shelter and suggested that they hitch the dogs and start traveling toward the west...just in case the ice might get close enough for them to make it to shore. Travel was slow at first because it was too dark to see rough places in the ice. After a night of darkness the dawning light was a great help.

The outline of the land was soon visible. Sam was glad that they had not passed Cape Nome during the night. He followed fairly close to the edge of the open water but not close enough to be unsafe. They could see Cape Nome was clearly ahead and to the west. When they were almost opposite, there was a lot of loose broken ice floating between them and the shore.

"Quickly, let's put the teams together and try for it," yelled Sam.

Hurriedly one sled was cut loose and the teams put together, with Sam's team in the lead. Sam decided to test the slush by walking on it. He tied a rope around his waist, fastened the other end to the sled, and then he started to walk. But it was too risky—he fell into the cold, slushy water. He quickly pulled on the rope, and his friend did his best on the other end, but it was hard to get out of the water. He finally did.

When the point of the ice they were on was about to pass the old shore ice, there was a space of broken ice and slush slowly moving up and down. As the main piece of ice they were on advanced, the pressure was so great it compressed these floating pieces of slush and ice as it forcefully pushed onward to the west. Sam knew this would not last much longer because of the speed at which it was moving. Soon there would be no hope, for their piece of ice would be out in the open Bering Sea with no land close by. Death would surely claim them.

"Let's go for it!" Sam shouted, hoping to cover his fear.

Both men yelled to their dogs as each grabbed the handlebar on their side of the sled, giving one sledrunner to each man. The dogs seemed to understand the seriousness of this situation, as all eagerly rushed forward. Some fell into soft slush but were pulled out by the others whose footing happened to be on a piece of solid ice.

Their hearts were filled with fear and hope, Sam and his friend kept hollering for the dogs to go faster. Every foot covered, as the dogs pulled the sled across the slush and chunks of ice, brought hope to both men. They knew that it was their dogs' frantic rush of speed that kept them and their sled above the soft, slushy ice. If the dogs stopped, the men would go down to certain death.

When the brave lead dog reached the solid shore ice he dug his claws in, pulling even harder until all the dogs and the sled were safely on the solid ice. Sam stopped the dogs and rushed forward to praise and give a quick pat to each dog as he headed for his lead dog. He knelt beside this brave, obedient dog with his arm around its neck and glanced back. He froze in this position . . . the piece of ice on which they had spent the night was drifting free with a span of dark green water between it and the pieces of broken ice and slush they had crossed.

Both men felt weak. Had they delayed just minutes, it would have been too late. Sam held his lead dog tighter, as he offered up his silent praise and thanks to God. He probably could not have spoken, had he tried. Sam looked again in disbelief and wonder at the piece of ice on which they had been so miserably trapped. Now it drifted free on the green-tinged waters of the Bering Sea. He knew that, as it drifted further from land, it would be hit with yet stronger winds, which would soon break it to pieces.

Ignoring his wet clothes, Sam stood and made his way back to the sled, petting and praising all the dogs again.

The two men looked at each other, smiled, then shook hands. Sam knew he and his friend were not out of danger. Both were wet and

Sam at the cabin he stayed in at Kiana Creek. The photo shows his missing right fingers. He is pictured with his faithful lead dog. Photographer unknown.

cold, and their clothing was beginning to freeze. They started driving for the nearest settlement, Nome, hoping to reach it before they became too frostbitten from their ice-cold clothes. Soon they met an Eskimo and his dog team. Word had already reached this man—he knew that two men had been taken out by the ice. Those on shore kept a lookout, although they had no hope as no one had ever before lived to return. He looked at them in disbelief, quickly noting their frozen clothes. He said, "Follow me, to friend nearby." At the cabin they were welcomed with dry clothes, hot coffee, and food, all freely given. The man who led them took care of and fed their dogs. Sam never forgot their kindness.

In the years that followed, Sam's lead dog became his companion, sharing the cabin with him at night.

Word traveled to the little settlements about these two men who were taken overnight on a piece of drifting ice that broke loose and drifted for many miles before briefly passing by the very tip of solid ice in front of Cape Nome, making it possible for them to become the first known men to make it back to land. Because of this they were looked upon as special by some of the older residents.

14

Eating Oogruk

Sam and his friend Carlisle, another prospector from the old country, would visit with the native people of Chiukak whenever they felt like driving the twelve or so miles. Sam liked these friendly, happy people and thought that he would try to help them learn more English words and also educate them in some of his customs.

He decided that the first step would be to explain that after cutting some things with a knife the white man would always wipe the knife clean before cutting something else. Most of the villagers had learned very few English words. That's why Sam and Carlisle decided to demonstrate with their own knife. Their friends nodded in understanding.

On their next visit to the village Sam and Carlisle entered their friends' home and found them all sitting around in a circle on the floor with a large pot of freshly cooked oogruk meat in the center. Their friends motioned for them to come in and asked if they would like to have a piece of the meat to eat. Sam and his friend thought why not. It looked clean, hot, and freshly cooked and it smelled good!

"Yes, please," they said as they nodded their heads. Both men had agreed beforehand to always say the proper English words when talking to these friendly people.

The woman who had been cutting off pieces of meat with the Eskimo knife—called ulu—bent forward to cut off a piece of meat, but then she stopped. These were the men who always wiped their knife after they cut something. She would not insult them by using an unwiped knife so she hurriedly looked around for something to wipe the knife with. The only thing handy was a used dog harness made from white man's cotton webbing. She grabbed it, then used it as she carefully wiped the ulu. With a smile she proceeded to cut two pieces of meat for the white men, wiping the ulu after cutting each piece.

Graciously Sam and his friend said, "Thank you." Sam thought the meat was tender and tasted as good as it smelled. As time passed Sam became good friends with the people of this little village.

15

Two Helpless Women

While visiting with his friends at Chiukak Sam heard about two women at the village of Rocky Point who had become bedridden and were, as the villagers said, "sick...no walk anymore." One was a young woman who had a small boy fathered by a white man who had left the country; the other was a woman about the same age. They were childhood friends. Until this happened they had been considered the most healthy and active women of the village.

While driving back to his cabin Sam pondered why two young women were unable to walk. Were they like the people said—beyond help? He checked his uncle's books to see if maybe they could be helped. He decided to see these two before coming to a decision.

A few days later he prepared to make the long trip, leaving at daybreak and arriving a little past noon. He was directed to Inerluk's inne. Kiachook greeted him, leading the way to where Nedercook and her friend lay—they really were bedridden. Sam noted that they were not plump like the other young people at the village. He asked them as many questions as he dared. "Four more days and I will come back. I will bring something for the women," he told Kiachook as he prepared to leave. Glancing at Nedercook he smiled, but there was no answering smile, just an indifferent stare.

After Sam left, Nedercook wondered if this man would really come back—she thought of the one who did not—still, something about this one seemed different. There was no doubt in Kiachook's mind. She knew this was a good, honorable man...she just knew!

It took Sam the rest of the day and part of the evening to make it back to his cabin. He was tired, and so were the dogs. He looked in his uncle's medical books searching for an answer. "Malnourished and bordering on scurvy" kept coming to mind.

Sam was back at Inerluk's home in four days. He had two cases of canned tomatoes and two containers of pills. Placing a case of tomatoes beside each woman's bed, he explained to Kiachook that what he brought was only for Nedercook and her companion. He asked her to make sure that no one else took the white pills. (Later in her life Minnie did not know if the pills were vitamin C, aspirin, or something else; she remembered only that they were not big and they were white.) Sam brought two can openers and two spoons. He opened the boxes and showed Nedercook and her companion how to open a can of tomatoes. He handed Nedercook a can and the opener and asked her to open one. In her weakened condition it was a struggle, but she did it. He was afraid that the women would not eat the tomatoes as they were, so he had a small container of sugar for each, and he explained that if the tomatoes tasted too sour to sprinkle just a little sugar on the tomatoes. (After this experience, before eating canned tomatoes, she would always sprinkle on just a little sugar.)

He told the women to take one of the pills. "Do not chew them, just swallow whole with water or take with the tomatoes." He made sure they also understood "only one can of tomatoes a day, and only one of the little pills a day—no more." He stressed it to all of them: "Just one a day of each—the tomatoes and the pill." He said he would come back in about two weeks to see how they were doing.

These were busy days for Sam and the weeks passed quickly. When he returned to the village he was pleased to see a little improvement in both women. He checked each container of pills to see if they were using them as instructed. He said he would come back later on with more. As he was ready to go he smiled at Nedercook. This time there was a small smile on her face.

Sam returned as promised. He brought more pills to take with the canned tomatoes. This time he was pleased to see the women were sitting up and looking so much better. He told them how happy he was to see their improvement. He also let them know that this would be his last trip because the snow was melting. Travel would be too hard on his dogs. He hoped they would continue to improve. If they came to his part of the country, he told them, stop by and let him know how they were. Sam did not charge them anything for his help. Kiachook was very appreciative and she would have liked to pay him, but they had nothing. She offered to make him mukluks or do any kind of sewing. Sam politely refused. All he wanted was to have the two walking again. This time, as he left, they waved and smiled.

Nedercook and her friend were soon walking. By the time the willow leaves and other greens were out they were well enough to gather them. They remembered what the man with missing fingers had said—to eat of their natural foods, especially the wild willow leaves, greens, berries, fish, meat, and when available they could add white man's food.

Unbeknownst to Sam, his reputation as a healer grew. This reputation stayed with him for a long time. Many years later Eskimos from Golovin or White Mountain would come to ask for his help whenever a family member did not recover as they should, or if someone was sick for no reason.

16

Working at
Port Safety Roadhouse

As time passed Kiachook became less active. She did not go out for the more difficult hunts. Whenever her native food was hard to get she often had coffee and sugar instead of the wild Hudson's Bay tea leaves that she used to gather each fall and in the spring. As she aged her eyesight began to fail. Her abdomen seemed to increase in size, and she also had a problem with piles. She did not know how to treat either condition. Even if a doctor could have helped her she was not about to let a stranger examine her.

Minnie (Nedercook now used her Christian name) decided that it was best to move back to Golovin. Kiachook and little J.D., who was not so little anymore, went with her. While living at Golovin, J.D. attended school. Minnie kept busy sewing skins for money or for trade at the store. She also learned how to bake bread from an old prospector. She enjoyed this and took pride in it.

The woman who owned and operated the Port Safety Roadhouse heard from several travelers about Minnie and the way she was left with a child. Being a compassionate and understanding woman she

Doll made by Nedercook of stone and dressed in otter parka with pants made of otter and squirrel. Courtesy University of Alaska Museum of the North, Ethnology and History Collection, cat. no. UA65-006-0001. Photo by Candace Smith.

Inset: Edna Wilder holding dolls made by her mother, Nedercook. Photo by Robert Wilder.

sent word to Golovin that she would like to have Minnie come to work for her. Minnie moved her mother and son back to Solomon, where they would be nearer to her job. They also had relatives living there.

Working under the guidance of this good woman, Minnie learned how to properly make a bed, clean rooms, do dishes, and wash and iron clothes. (To iron she had to place a flat iron on the wood-burning stove, remove the wooden handle from the iron while it warmed, place the wooden handle onto another flat iron that was already hot on the stove, and use it until it lost its pressing heat. Then she returned the cooled iron to the stove to reheat.) She also learned how to sweep the dining room floor with a broom and not cause the dust to rise—it was the custom with the old-timers to sprinkle damp coffee grounds or tea leaves over the wooden floor before sweeping. She also learned how to bake pies, cakes, cookies, doughnuts, and a considerable amount of bread, and to cook many of the white man's dishes. She would set the tables and later clear them, and carry food from the kitchen to the tables. She was also taught about money and how to make the proper change.

Quite a number of the travelers coming from Nome would stop at the roadhouse with their dog teams, usually having coffee and a hot lunch. Many coming from longer distances would spend the night. Roadhouses in Alaska during that time would provide food and a sort of a bunkhouse where the travelers could sleep, and a barn to house the dog teams overnight. This building had many low stalls with chains fastened to the inside of each open stall. The chain was short and allowed the dog's face or snout to just reach to the outer edge of the stall, thereby preventing a fight with the neighboring dog. A dog had enough room to eat the dried salmon that was standard dog food in those days or lie down on the dry hay to sleep and rest. Each dog's harness was placed on the flat top above the stall. Dogs that had to travel for long distances over crusted snow would develop sore or bleeding feet, so dog boots had to be used but removed for the night and dried if damp.

The Port Safety Roadhouse was a double-story building. Rooms for travelers were on the second floor. The first floor contained the kitchen, dining and utility room, storage room, the proprietor's room, and two rooms for the help.

Most men in Alaska had respect for all women, but once in a while a man with different priorities would stop by. One particular customer thought that he might be able to take advantage of the young native woman who took care of the rooms and waited on tables. When he was sure that she was in his room making the bed and doing other chores, on some pretext he re-entered the room. Minnie was wary of his unexpected appearance, and made sure to keep the bed between them. After they had circled the bed a few times, he waited until she was across the narrow side, lunged at her, and grabbed her by the arm. While holding her arm tight he leaped over the bed and grabbed at her body. She fought like a tigress. When he did not let her go, Minnie screamed as loud as she could while she kicked and fought with the man. Her boss had told her what to do if anyone tried to take advantage of her. Since the building was not soundproof she could easily hear her. The door flew open and the owner was in the room before the man could harm Minnie. Looking him straight in the eye, with a voice of authority she told him to never, ever bother her help again. Grabbing his belongings he hurriedly left.

Minnie worked several years for this kind woman. One spring the woman got a good offer from a man who wanted to buy the roadhouse. She decided to sell and return to her hometown in the States— "the Outside," as it was called at that time. Minnie did not like the new owner. She decided to return to Rocky Point with J.D. and Kiachook. After spending some time with relatives at Solomon they traveled down the coast in an umiak, stopping at Bluff City to visit some friends. Sam was there to leave a letter to be mailed. He was very pleased with Minnie's complete recovery but was shocked at the change in Kiachook. From her appearance he concluded that she had a very large tumor in her abdomen. Because it was very obvious, he mentioned it to Minnie. Kiachook had difficulty moving about. An operation seemed the only hope for her now, but she did not want one.

Kiachook realized that it would be too hard for her to get to her home at Rocky Point, and decided that it would be best to return to Solomon and the cabin in which she had spent the last few years. Making the trip back was harder on Kiachook than Minnie had anticipated. Kiachook had a difficult time for the next few weeks while Minnie did her best to take care of her.

One morning while Minnie was fixing their breakfast, Kiachook called Minnie to her bedside. As Minnie held her mother's hand, she heard her softly say, "My daughter, today I take the long sleep." Then she closed her eyes.

That was Kiachook's last day. She was buried high on a beach at Solomon.

17

One Way to Get a Wife

With the passing of time Minnie's thoughts turned more and more to the kind man with the missing fingers. When Sam heard of Kiachook's passing he decided to make a trip to Solomon, express his sympathy, and in general see how she was doing. He would have to wait until there was enough snow for dog team travel.

One Eskimo man and one white man had been trying to get Minnie to say yes to marriage. She cared for neither and told them so. However, both persisted in their efforts to change her mind. The more they tried to convince her the more she disliked both men.

After Sam arrived at Solomon it did not take him long to realize he was not leaving without Minnie and J.D. He knew that he would have to work hard, especially during the spring, summer, and fall months in order to pay off a debt he owed on the mining claims he was working, as well as to buy food and other things that were needed.

He carefully explained all this to Minnie before he asked her if under these conditions she would be willing to come back with him as his wife-to-be, and then wait until sometime in the winter, or next winter, when they would be able to drive by dog team to

Minnie and her son George standing at the corner of the
cabin that Sam built. Photographer unknown.

Unalakleet, Alaska, where there was a commissioner to officially perform the marriage.

He asked Minnie if she would be his wife. As he put his arms around her, Minnie felt a deep, peaceful calm fill her being as if she had suddenly found refuge from a storm; she felt safe in Sam's arms.

"Yes," was her soft reply.

When Sam arrived home he promptly wrote to the commissioner at Unalakleet, explaining about Minnie and her son and his intentions to marry her and adopt J.D. In his letter, Sam said that he wanted to do the right thing by this fine Alaskan woman, and not have a common-law marriage as some of the early arrivals to Alaska did, explaining about having to wait until the following year or next until he could pay off some of his debt.

Minnie liked the cabin Sam had built, which had a big porch in front. For the first time since the death of her mother, a feeling of peace and happiness filled Minnie's heart. J.D. was happy too; he liked being

To the right of the pole in the background is the series of cabins Sam built when he moved his family closer to the bluff. This was Minnie's home until Sam passed away. Photo by Edna Wilder.

around Sam. Minnie did not mind waiting for an official marriage. Sam had taken her into his home, and she felt secure that he would not leave her. She cooked, kept the home clean, hunted, and picked the wild berries when she could. She had little J.D. with her. Life was good.

18

Orphaned Reindeer

Sam had built a nice cozy log cabin with a closed-in porch that was now their home. It was located about an eighth of a mile from the cliff and about fifty feet south of the winter trail that he used to haul wood or logs from Kiana Creek and Long Beach. From there the trail continued on behind the Big Mountain, where it joined the regular winter trail or the mail trail, as it was called, which passed just above the head of this creek.

One summer day Minnie walked this trail to Twin Creeks, as she often did. Today she was checking on how the wild berries were doing. On the way she saw a mother reindeer with a calf; the mother looked like she had something wrong with her foot. When Minnie told Sam about it he thought it sounded like a clubfoot and he said the deer would probably die from it. For the rest of the summer she would make it a point every now and then to see how the mother was doing. The foot kept getting bigger and the mother was not moving around like she should, and before snow the mother reindeer died. Minnie felt sorry for the young orphan, and stopped by to see it quite often. The young reindeer seemed lonely and on this particular day it started to

BLACK CHIEF BLUFF, NEAR BLUFF, ALASKA.

*Black Chief Bluff, near Bluff, Alaska, on Norton Sound.
Late nineteenth or early twentieth century. Courtesy
Anchorage Museum at Rasmuson Center, General
Photograph File, image no. AMRC-b65-18-755.*

follow her home, but after a short distance it ran back to where its mother's decaying body lay. When Minnie told Sam, they decided it would be best to go and cover the remains so that whatever had killed her would not spread.

When Minnie next passed by that way the young reindeer followed her home. Sam and Minnie both felt sorry for it and offered it some food. That night it lay down in front of the window where the light from the kerosene lamp could be seen. Next morning it was still there. After this each evening they would hear a thump by the window as the deer settled in for the night. The orphaned reindeer refused to leave and would follow them wherever they went. At first the dogs did quite a lot of barking but soon they seemed to accept it.

One day Sam was going to walk to Bluff and get the mail—since there was no snow it was delivered by boat. The reindeer saw him leaving and started to follow him. Sam thought it would go back but it kept following him. When he got to the roadhouse and was going to go in, it wanted to go in with him. The owners said, "Let him in," and it walked in. After this Sam decided it was not a good idea to take the reindeer to Bluff because the dogs there were not friendly. Sam rigged up a collar so that it could be kept at home if needed, and be turned loose as soon as he returned.

When the ice froze over on the Bering Sea, they fished for tomcod through holes that Sam cut, placing dead fish a few feet from the open hole in the ice. The young reindeer soon approached the catch and started eating the fresh unfrozen fish. This took Sam by surprise, but the reindeer seemed to like it and did not get sick, so after that they often would let it eat some fish. As time passed the reindeer became a real pet and would follow them anywhere—it would go with Sam and the dog team when he hauled wood from Kiana Creek.

One day when Sam and Minnie were enjoying a late lunch and the reindeer was loose, their dogs started to bark. Looking out of the window, they saw a dog team approaching from the direction of Kiana

Creek. As it was about to pass, the dogs saw the reindeer and rushed from the trail, dragging the sled with the driver hanging onto the handlebars as he kept yelling and cussing. The reindeer seemed to know this was not a friendly bunch of dogs, and to get away it ran in an ever-widening circle around the house as the dogs paid no attention to the man's yelling and cussing as he clung to the sled. When another team showed up and blocked the reindeer's way, it turned and ran along the trail toward Bluff, with both teams now in pursuit.

Sam and Minnie thought the reindeer was trying to save them by leading these harmful dogs away from them. Later they learned that the dog teams were in a race and were going back to Nome, from Golovin. When the lead team neared Kiana Creek and saw Sam's fresh wood-hauling trail, he took it, instead of going on up Kiana Creek to join the mail trail. The next team followed, and thus both lost their lead in the race.

That night the reindeer did not come back to sleep by the window. When Sam went to Bluff he learned that the reindeer had run until it was two miles from Solomon. It was dark by then, so when it saw a light shining from a window in a log cabin a short distance from the trail, the exhausted animal had gone to it, frightening the occupants as it flopped down in front of it. The two prospectors, unaware that this was a tame reindeer, shot it.

19

Sorrow and Grief

Minnie *loved to beach-comb.* One day, when the snow was gone from the beaches Minnie was walking along last fall's high tide line, where unexpected things could be found. She spotted a child's bow in such good condition she decided to take it home for J.D., recalling the one she had found and given to her brother Oolark shortly before he had drowned while stalking a seal. J.D. was happy and with some help from Sam he soon had arrows good enough to get rabbits or small animals, and his marksmanship was improving rapidly.

Kiana Creek had a nice sandy, curving beach in front of the little creek. The beach began at the end of the cliffs to the west, then curved in toward the creek before continuing on for possibly a quarter of a mile east to where a bunch of very large rocks jutted into the sea. Beyond this was another little beach, which continued for about a quarter of a mile to where the cliffs began again. Further on a tall, large rock stood out in the water a hundred feet or more from the shore. Murres, puffins, kittiwake gulls, and other sea birds nested on it. This rock was almost a perfect square so people naturally called it "Square Rock."

Beyond it was a beach about nine miles long, ending where the little village of Chiukak used to be before the big flu killed almost all of the people living there. The survivors moved away, leaving many of the typical teepee-like graves high on the beach. From there the sea water took over, going around the cliffs of Rocky Point toward Golovin Bay.

Sam and Minnie would put their salmon net in the sea about halfway between the outlet of Kiana Creek and the cliffs to the west of this curving beach. This was a good place to catch salmon. They used a rowboat to set the net out, and later to check for fish by reaching down over the side of the boat and grabbing the float line as it bobbed up and down with the rise and fall of the water. Lifting it to the edge of the boat while holding onto the line, they followed it by going hand over hand. If a fish was in the net, they would lift the net and fish so that when the untangled fish was free it would drop into the bottom of the boat. Doing this, they could remove the fish without out the trouble of pulling the net to shore and then having to reset it with the rowboat.

Salmon favored this part of the water, but so did seals and especially the large sea lions, which the natives feared should they be out in their kayaks because these large mammals would attack a kayak, tipping it and causing the occupant to drown. All this spring, every so often Minnie had the feeling of imaginary tears rolling down her cheeks, and she wondered why.

One evening the man who let Sam stay in one of his cabins during the year that he lost his fingers in a gun accident at Kiana Creek stopped by Sam's home. He told Sam that he needed help for a day, and asked if Sam would be able to help him. Sam was there early the next morning and the two men worked until noon. After a brief lunch they began again.

Around four in the afternoon young J.D., who was about twelve years of age, came to where the men were working. He asked permission to go out in the little dory to remove the salmon from his mother's net. He had done this many times before. Sam, who was busy trying to help finish the work before evening, said, "OK, but be careful."

"May I please use your gum boots?" J.D. asked the man that Sam was helping. (During this period, hip boots were called thus.)

"You can... if you will bring them back when you are through," replied the Swede. The two men continued working, hoping to finish the job before the day's end.

When some time had passed and J.D. had not returned with the gum boots, Sam became worried. He and his friend walked down to the creek's mouth, where they could see the net. What they saw was the overturned dory washing in the waves by the edge of the beach. Rushing down they righted the boat. It was empty. They hollered for little J.D. but there was no answer. The oars had washed ashore a little further down the beach. The men rowed out to the net, lifting it and looking closely for any sign of the boy. There was none. They rowed around peering into the sea water, but there was no sign of J.D.

Minnie was at home baking bread when Sam came and told her. She was terribly upset and immediately took off for Kiana Creek. Minnie had pulled the net ashore by the time Sam arrived with a dragging device. He and his friend used this as best they could, giving the area a thorough dragging until the increasing wind made it too rough. They walked the beaches calling J.D.'s name, but there was no answer.

Residents of Bluff came and joined the search. All they could do was walk the beaches and look to the sea for any floating object. A day later, when the sea became a little calmer, they used their small boats to go around searching the beaches under the cliffs, with no results.

Minnie was devastated. She walked the shores and looked. She walked above the clifftops. Using her brass telescope she scanned the beaches and the rough sea. Each floating log gave her hope until the telescope focused upon it. At night, exhausted, she would lie with her hand cupped behind her right ear so that she could hear better if her boy called. She could not give up hoping that he might still be alive ... maybe he was hurt and trying to get home, or stuck on some beach. She did not want to miss his call for help. The effect of sleeping thus for so long made her right ear protrude more than the other ear.

Minnie spent her days grieving and searching. Eventually Sam had to go back to work. In the evening after a day of hard work he would walk the beaches, looking. Three weeks passed, and little J.D. was still missing. Then another week passed and as usual Sam left after work to search the beaches for the boy. While walking a beach about two miles east of Kiana Creek, Sam found the body of little J.D. It had washed up by some rocks and driftwood, on the last beach before Square Rock. The body was so decayed that he had to leave it and go back for some sheets and help to carry it. He walked about four miles to get home— Sam walked this after a hard day of work. When Sam told Minnie that he was walking to Bluff to get help, she rushed out the door on her way to the beach, thinking of holding her boy in her arms. Little J.D. had been in the sea too long, and his body was decayed. In her rush to hold him she reached to encircle his body and her fingers punctured through his skin and flesh. In horror she looked and then she saw the sea lice that clung around all the open areas of his skin. The odor of decay was very strong. Her grief was terrible to see.

Sam, with help of other men, carefully rolled the body in clean white sheets. Then they carried the body along the beaches and around the jutting rocks that separated the beaches, up the steep climb at the beginning of the cliffs by Kiana Creek to the summer trail that wound along near the edge of the clifftop, then over the little hills until they reached the hill that was about a half mile from Sam's home. It had a good view of the little valley. Friends came from Bluff City and took turns at digging a grave, which was soon ready.

Minnie was so distraught, Sam feared for her sanity. He decided to take her to Solomon, where her sister and her last remaining relatives lived. Since he had to work he thought that if she lived with them for a month or so their concern and constant companionship would help her to accept the death of her son. Sam suffered misgivings about the accident, and about having to leave Minnie during this time of sorrow and grief. However, he had the responsibility for their existence. In order to do that he had to earn a living for them during the short mining season.... He could not do both.

Fortunately for Minnie, their first son, a boy, was born on the thirty-first of July while she was still with her relatives. This was a blessing because it helped her. Caring for little Samuel was good therapy for Minnie. Although the hurt remained in both their hearts, their love was strong enough to reunite them in harmony at the end of the mining season.

Winter came and went, bringing another summer season. Sam mined and did the needed chores at home. Minnie cooked, hunted, fished, and picked wild berries for the table. She stored all the berries that they did not need that day in fifty- and one-hundred-pound wooden barrels. When available she liked the empty fifty-pound butter barrels because they always seemed so clean. (Back then butter was shipped in pound bricks stored in a large white sack, which was closed and placed in a wooden barrel filled with brine.) Sam had dug a hole large enough for several barrels, fairly close to the edge of the cliff where the cool breeze from the sea helped to keep the root cellar cool. When one barrel was full, Minnie would sprinkle a layer of sugar over the entire top, just enough to cover it white. Then she placed a clean white flour sack over the barrel and tied it securely. A wooden cover went on top. Kept cool and away from the sun, the berries never spoiled before they froze with the coming of winter. She also dug up wild roots (called Eskimo potatoes today). They were stored in sand or soil and the container was put in the shed until cold weather, then taken to the cellar. The cellar was a square hole beneath the floor of their home, with a ladder going down from a trap door.

Minnie became pregnant again around the time when there was much talk of the Halley's Comet expected appearance. When it did appear, Sam and Minnie saw it streaking across the sky. They decided to name the baby Halley after the comet. He was a happy, robust child. One day, when Halley had reached the age of walking and investigating all things as children love to do, Sam was hauling wood by dog team from the west end of long beach. He was gone several hours. Shortly after the noon meal Halley suddenly started to fuss as if he did not feel good. Soon after he started to cry as if he was in pain. Minnie tried to comfort him and asked where it hurt, but he was too young to tell her in words. She was not sure but figured that his pain was from his stomach. His cries became worse, and while crying he suddenly died.

Minnie had fed him some cooked rice that day and wondered if she had done wrong by feeding him too much rice. He had eaten rice many times before and there was never any trouble.

Sam could find no answer to this sudden death, unless possibly Halley had picked up something and, as children often do, put it in his mouth and swallowed it as he was moving about their home.

Death this sudden and so unexpected was hard on both Sam and Minnie. Life became a struggle for each as they lived through the following days. Halley was buried on the hill beside J.D.

Miners and prospectors who had no time to bake but wanted to buy loaves of homemade bread came to the Tuckers' home, asking if Minnie would bake and sell them bread. Sam thought this might be a healing thing for Minnie to do, so he agreed. She sold a loaf for twenty-five cents, bringing in a small income. They bought dark and white flour in one-hundred-pound gunnysacks.

For leavening she made her own liquid yeast and stored it in a large jar, which lasted a long time. In the evening she would mix a soft batter and add a cup of this mix. In the morning she added salt, sugar, shortening, and enough flour to make a workable bread dough. The miners also liked it when she would use bacon drippings for shortening. It took the greater part of a day to get the bread ready for baking.

Minnie enjoyed doing it, and the compliments from the miners made her feel good, which helped her during this time of loss. Although Minnie enjoyed making bread, she decided it took too much time away from fishing and getting meat and berries for food, so she decided that one year of this was enough.

20

Two Men Name a Baby

A *white woman who was spending* the winter at Bluff was expecting her first child, and naturally she was quite apprehensive about having a baby without a doctor. Her husband mentioned his wife's fears to Sam, expressing his regret that they lived so far apart and wondering if they could call upon Minnie's help when the time came.

Sam decided that since Minnie was also expecting, it might be wise for them to move to his little cabin at Bluff, at least until after Minnie's delivery. That way both women would be near each other.

Minnie would walk to the white woman's home nearly every other day, then each day as the time of her delivery approached. Early one morning a messenger came to say the baby was coming. Minnie stayed by the woman's side all day. The birth seemed hard. Unlike the women of Minnie's village this woman did not kneel to deliver her child but preferred to lie in bed. She also did some screaming, but eventually a fine little girl was born. The woman was very thankful for Minnie's help and offered to pay her. Minnie refused pay for doing something that any woman in her village would have done without thought of a reward.

Sam decided that they should remain at the Bluff cabin until after Minnie had their baby, which was due soon. Early one morning, after Sam had gone to get a load of wood, Minnie knew that the baby was coming. She glanced at her sleeping son. Although there was no one to help her, she was not afraid. Childbirth was a natural occurrence not to be feared by her people. Quickly she made preparations and then, as was the custom of her people, she went to her knees.

This baby did not want to come easily. After some time Minnie reached down and felt two little feet that would come no further. She made up her mind quickly, and gently she pulled... soon the baby was free. To her joy it was a little girl. She had dark brown hair and compared to their sleeping son, this baby's skin was much lighter.

Sam wondered what to name the baby. Minnie knew what Eskimo name she would give her—Kiachook, after her mother, and she would also give her a second name, Oolark, after her brother and J.D.

When Sam's friend Carlisle stopped by to see the baby, Sam decided that this was a good time to officially name her. Carlisle had a sister called Edna. He loved his sister but like Sam's sister she lived across the far seas. Carlisle asked if the baby could be named after his sister Edna.

Sam had a sister that he loved called Maude. So they asked Minnie if she liked the names. She did.

Sam prepared a cup of water for the naming. Carlisle, while holding back the tears in his eyes, sprinkled a few drops of water on the baby's head; she did not cry. In a voice filled with emotion he said, "I hereby christen you Edna after my sister and Maude after Sam's sister." Then he broke into tears and cried.

Life continued on a happier note as spring arrived. Sam worked the mine while Minnie took care of the home. She gathered fresh greens with little Edna riding near the hood of her parka. She hunted the wild game for meat, fished, and picked berries.

Minnie takes her daughter berry picking after finding out she will not go to England for school. Edna is embarrassed to be photographed as she eats a sandwich. The beautiful wooden bucket was made by Inerluk for Minnie when she was a girl. Photo by Lena Bahnke.

Using an old treadle sewing machine Minnie would sew clothes for the boy and dresses for herself and the little girl. She needed no patterns for this because after years spent hand-sewing furs, she could look at a Montgomery Ward catalog for a dress style she liked and the finished dress would be just like it.

One day, when little Edna was nearly three, Sam looked at her and wondered how he could give her an education, because the nearest grade school was at Golovin—a long day's travel by dog team in the winter if the weather was good.

He thought of his sister Maude in England. If they sent Edna to her by steamship and sent money by mail, she would see that Edna was enrolled in a good school. The only problem was that the expense of travel back and forth was beyond their means, so once Edna was gone, they would not be able to see her until after she graduated. By then she would be a young woman. Sam explained the advantage of a good education to Minnie, and since it seemed like years before little Edna would leave, Minnie did not seem too concerned. In the following years Sam worked hard, and managed to save enough money by the time little Edna was nearly seven. As the end of the summer drew near, Minnie realized that after this she would not be able to see their daughter for many years. Edna accompanied her on walks to harvest food, and both were enjoying each other's company. Suddenly Minnie could not bear to think of not seeing her every day. She put her arms around her daughter, and with tears in her eyes she asked Sam to keep her with them.

This decision was not hard for Sam. He decided to send money to his sister and have her mail some books to them. He would help their daughter learn to read, write, and do arithmetic.

21

Big Flu

Sam was outdoors sawing wood when he noticed a dark object coming along the winter trail from Bluff, which he assumed was a man. Minnie got her brass telescope.

"Mickey Powers," she said as she turned to go back inside to finish the bread-baking. Sam figured it must be something urgent to bring his friend who lived over five miles away, so he started up the trail to meet him. Mickey with his Irish brogue said, "It's the big flu epidemic. Word is that it has struck the native people at Solomon, nearly wiping them out. So because of your Minnie I thought I'd better come and warn ye." Then he continued, "Before she hears it from a stranger."

With this said, Mickey turned to start the long walk home but he stopped and asked, "Is there any word you wish me to deliver?"

"Yes," Sam replied, "Would you please give a message to the people who operated the roadhouse?" Pausing for a moment before continuing, he said, "Tell them I'm moving my family to our cabin on the hillside at Bluff. We will stay in quarantine for at least a month, or longer if necessary. I'll put my big trunklike wood box by the old engine near the creek. Any mail or messages may be left there. I will fix a white flag to raise if we should have trouble. It will be easily seen from the door of the roadhouse." Sam expressed his appreciation and thanks and added, "Because she has already suffered too many losses, I'll not mention the deaths to Minnie until we are sure her relatives are among the dead."

Sam walked back and told Minnie that Mickey had come to warn them about a big flu epidemic that was spreading along the coast. He said that they would get ready and move right away to his cabin at Bluff, where they would stay until the danger had passed.

Hurriedly while it was still daylight, things were loaded into Sam's basket sled. The first load would have bedding and anything that getting a little cold would not hurt. He would get the fire going at the Bluff cabin and then come back alone for all perishables.

They remained isolated from other people at the hillside cabin, but were free to wander around the hills and to the home they had left. From their window they could observe the activity going on around the roadhouse and see anyone who brought something to the box. Because of the high winds that often blew Sam had secured it to an old engine frame.

Staying away like this they escaped the flu. Minnie's relatives at Solomon were not so lucky. From her family only one niece survived; she later married and moved to White Mountain.

22

Strange Noise

One afternoon while the two oldest children were playing near the edge of the cliff they heard the strangest noise. It seemed to be coming from the east behind the hill where the graves were. Both started to run for home to tell their mother about this strange noise that was getting louder and louder.

Sam was in a hole digging to check the gravel for gold in a new area of the mine where it was quite rocky. He had just removed a rather large rock from the side of the hole that he had been working on. Suddenly he heard a strange noise. He cocked his head to listen nearer to the opening, wondering what could be down in this hole that would make a noise like that. As the sound grew louder he realized that it was not coming from the hole but from the sky to the east.

Then he knew—it was the Around the World Fliers! He ran out and up the bank, and removing his hat he began waving it like some kind of a crazy man. By the time the children reached Minnie, she had already heard it. She knew immediately. Sam had told her about the first airplanes that would be flying around the world and that they would be flying along the coast. She ran outside and watched as they flew by.

Most of the people had never seen or heard of an airplane before. Many had no knowledge that such machines even existed. One Eskimo woman was picking berries beside a little knoll. When she heard the buzzing drone of the planes she was petrified, sure that there was a devil, or "dorn-ruk," under the knoll, and that it was about to come out and get her. She was so frightened that the devil would come out at any moment that she could not take her eyes from the knoll as the sound grew louder. In her fright she did not even see the planes pass by.

It was said that there was one woman who was considered completely deaf. She was picking berries and smelled something different. She happened to look up in time to see the airplanes before they went out of sight. Two men from Solomon, Kootogon and his friend Arpuk, were out hunting at the same time. When they heard the sound of the airplanes, Kootogon called to his companion, "Arpuk, hold my head!"

23

The Owl's Good-bye

Minnie *became pregnant again*. This time she seemed to be gaining a little more weight than normal. Sam was concerned, especially when she continued to do the physical things that he had cautioned her against, physical things that the average woman might never do. Minnie, however, was strong-willed at times, and she would lift or carry things that she probably should not.

One day while she was home alone, she delivered to her shock not one but two little still-born boys. They were well formed and had nice features. This was a sad experience for Sam and Minnie to live through.

The twins were laid to rest together in one small grave beside J.D. and little Halley.

Time passed and eventually Minnie became pregnant again. Her labor was not easy. Sam was quite concerned for her. After several hours he was very relieved when a healthy boy was born. Seeing how Minnie had suffered through this delivery and recalling the birth of the still-born twins, he feared that another pregnancy might take her life. The very thought that he might be the cause of Minnie's death was more than he could bear. Sam decided then and there that as much as he hated to, he must abstain from any action that might bring on another pregnancy.

They named this boy George Alfred. He seemed healthy and grew strong, playing with his brother and sister. When the children were older they would bring home young crippled gulls and baby murres that had fallen from their place on the cliff. Broken wings or legs were most common with the little kittiwake gulls, but twice they found an injured adult murre.

Sam showed the children how to put a splint on the wing or leg. The children learned fast and soon they did all the splinting. The first few times they would check with their father to see if it was properly done.

They cut fish into small pieces to feed them. After weeks of care the children carried the birds down the steep cliff to the edge of the sea water. Setting them down, they would stand back and watch the birds swim away.

One day in the early spring while out with their mother, the children found a gray-, brown-, and white-marked owl with a broken wing. It took a month of nursing before they could remove the splint. It did not take the owl long to fly. It circled their home twice and then flew north.

One late September evening just before dusk when they were all working outdoors, an owl that looked like the one they had helped flew by overhead. Then it turned back and circled their home three times before it continued on south. "It must be saying 'good-bye' and 'thank you' before leaving this part of Alaska," the children joyfully said. Their parents agreed.

24

Brave Woman

Sam had worked hard all summer digging out what he hoped was gold-bearing gravel and shoveling it into his wheelbarrow. He would pick up the handles, and as he balanced it and himself, he would push it along the twelve-inch planks that he had placed over piles of rock. Reaching the dump he would empty the wheelbarrow and return for more. He had quite a large pile, or dump as he called it, by the end of this unusually dry season.

This year he had missed the annual trip he usually took with the last mail boat to Nome for winter supplies. Next week's trip of the mail boat would be the last chance to get their winter's supply of groceries before freeze-up.

If he could get what gold he had prepared and a list of needed groceries to Solomon by the next day, it would just make it in time. Sam was wondering how they could get it there in time because he still had to get the rest of the gravel run through the sluice boxes and cleaned up before freeze-up in order to have money for the debt on the claim he was working on and other items.

Minnie offered to walk the many miles to Solomon next morning and take the grocery order and gold. Sam was pleased and wrote a note to the Shonnesys, who owned the roadhouse and the store.

Minnie left very early the next morning. She was in good shape and although it was a long, hard walk she made it just as darkness was falling. The Shonnesys were so happy to see Minnie, and they thought she was a very brave woman to walk all those miles alone. They treated her to dinner and gave her a room free of charge. Sam in his letter had asked them to deduct that from the gold she brought. But they thought a woman who did what Minnie had just done was special and needed to be given this treat.

Minnie returned home with gifts from Mrs. Shonnesy: apples, oranges, candy, and a pretty scarf for her head, as well as a list of all the groceries that were ordered for delivery with the next mail boat, a paid receipt for the groceries, and cash for the remaining gold. She had high praise for the Shonnesys' hospitality.

Minnie spent the remaining days gathering berries, because freeze-up would make them too soft for picking. When no other meat was available Minnie would use her brother's old 30-30 rifle to shoot a beluga, or as they were called then, "white whale." She would position herself near the cliff's edge, and as they passed in the sea south of her she would shoot one after it had surfaced and before it dove. If she shot too soon, before it inhaled air, it would sink. When she shot she did not miss.

She would always give whale steaks to the old prospectors, who relished the fresh meat. She cooked and then preserved the white muktuk in oil, hung the meat to dry, and saved some of the blubber to render into oil for winter use. The rest was saved for the dogs.

Whales often passed by in the sea below the cliff, which was about two hundred and fifty feet above sea level. From the kitchen window they could be seen coming as they surfaced, sometimes in little groups and at times just two or three. If they did not need one for food, Minnie would not shoot. She always enjoyed watching them because as they passed they could be seen as a white blur swimming underwater until they surfaced, unless it was just after a storm when the sea water was often murky for a day.

25

The Spirit Circled Her

Before Christmas Minnie would spend her spare time making mukluks, slippers, mittens, or whatever kind of fur piece she knew a friend would need. She also on the sly made new items for her family. When the children first asked what she was sewing, it just happened that she was making something for Mrs. Meegan. After that she was able to make their Christmas presents because the children figured she was sewing for Mrs. Meegan. After the children had gone to bed, Minnie would sew up little toy animals and dolls for them.

One winter evening Minnie was sitting on the floor, both legs straight out in front of her, sewing busily. Sam and Sam Jr. had gone to Bluff for the mail. During the winter the mail came once a week by dog team from Nome. The mail carrier usually arrived late in the afternoon or early evening. He would overnight at the Bluff roadhouse before going to Golovin, where he would overnight before making the return trip back to Nome with his twelve dogs. During peak mail runs he would have twenty-four dogs. If the mail was light for that trip he would often bring a passenger or two destined for Golovin or further.

Two pieces of beadwork made by Minnie. The bead-trimmed pocket
is used as a wall hanging. The oogruk skin was tanned with alder
bark to give it its red appearance. Photographer unknown.

The two younger children asked Minnie if they could go out and play. As always, she cautioned them to stay away from the edge of the cliff. They ran to the mouth of the creek. It was filled with hard drifted snow formed into dips by the strong winds, like little bathtubs of varying sizes. Each child picked a dip with a space of about ten feet separating them. They wanted to play the shooting stars game. Pulling up their parka hoods they lay on their backs and looked up at the stars. Whoever saw a shooting star first would yell, "I see one." The first one to say this could claim that shooting star. Coming back later they eagerly told their mother who saw the most shooting stars and about the one that had a long flaming tail as it seemed to arch across the sky before it suddenly went out. Minnie waited patiently until they were finished.

"While you were gone a spirit came, it circled around me," she said. "I could feel it as it moved around me, somehow it felt or made me think of someone I knew a long time ago." The children sensed their mother's uneasiness and did not question her.

Sam and Sam Jr. were late to return and Minnie began to worry. When they finally came Sam said they were late because of the man who had arrived with the mail carrier. He had come into the roadhouse and before the mail bag was opened for distribution, he suddenly died there in front of all the people who were waiting for their mail.

Minnie told Sam about the intense feeling she had of a certain man's presence as it circled and traveled around her. It seemed to be the one who years earlier had chased her around the bed at the roadhouse. When she mentioned his name, Sam exclaimed, "That was the name of the man who died!"

26

Crane

Minnie had not been hunting for fresh meat since the birds had nested and the young rabbits were little. This was a time for them to grow and they were not killed unless there was a real emergency. They were taken only after the berries began to ripen—by then they would be of adult size, which should be any day now.

Sam, who had never been other than strong and healthy since Minnie had known him, began to feel ill. Today he did not feel good at all and was lying in bed. Minnie figured that lack of fresh meat was probably the cause. She was wondering what she should do.

Hearing loud crane noises, she looked and saw two cranes flying by quite low. As she watched they set their wings and glided down behind a small rocky hill that they had named Fox Mountain because they had seen a fox there. Thinking that this was an answer to her problem, she picked up her old 30-30 rifle and shells and asked Sam Jr. to keep the children indoors until she returned. When she reached Fox Mountain she cautiously went to the top and slowly peeked around a large rock and saw two cranes out on the tundra. It would be a long shot. But she knew that if they saw her they would fly away.

Cranes had never landed there before, so she had to take this chance and hope that her aim would be good. Sliding the gun out beside the rock she carefully took aim. By then the cranes knew something was at the rocks and both were looking her way. They might take off any minute. She pressed the trigger. One crane fell while the other left. Minnie ran as fast she could. The crane was dead—the bullet had gone through its head, killing it instantly.

She cleaned it as soon as she got home and saved some of the blood, boiling it with the finely chopped heart and gizzard and adding the chopped liver a short time before it was done. While this was boiling gently, she added some finely chopped wild onions she had gathered. These grew along several of the sunny slopes near the cliff's edge. For a moment she was undecided, then she also tossed in a little oatmeal, pepper, and salt.

She fed some of this rich broth to Sam, telling him that he would get better, and that tomorrow she would fix some of the meat for him. Sam started feeling better. Next day she cooked the crane, and by then Sam's appetite was good. When an old-timer happened to stop by, he joined Sam and they both enjoyed a wonderful meal. The old-timer was very appreciative because he too had been out of meat for too long.

Sam recovered and continued to feel good.

Minnie would sometimes tell her children of the lucky rifle shot years ago that helped their father to get well. They thought it bordered on bragging.

27

No More Bluff City

During the early fall sometimes Minnie and her daughter would walk for about five miles to where they could cross over the hills at the divide, then down to the headwaters of a stream that drained on that side of the mountains toward the Golovin Bay flats. They followed it for several miles downstream because the fish were bigger as the water increased. There the fish would collect in larger pools.

Willows grew along the sides of the creek. They were not tall, and strong winds made them grow crooked, but Minnie would find one that was not too crooked, cut it down, and fasten a length of about four or five feet of white string. (In those days fifty-pound flour and sugar sacks and some other food bags were sewn with white thread in a chain stitch that easily unraveled. Minnie saved it for many uses.) To the end of the string she then tied a pin that was bent into the shape of a hook. After fixing these two fishing rods they would follow the stream as it increased in size until there were small pools of water were several trout and sometimes a grayling or two would be.

She tied on a small piece of bacon. When she did not have bacon she made a small ball of dough to use on the hook, but this fell from the hook quickly.

She showed her child how to catch a fish. Then she would clean this fish, and if they had only dough for bait, she would use a part of the fish's stomach for bait on the hook. This worked very well. They continued downstream fishing and laughing as one or the other would catch a larger fish, saying, "I just caught a whale."

When Minnie decided they had caught enough fish they built a small fire on a gravel bar, just big enough to boil water in a coffee can that had two holes punched in near the top, and a wire looped from one side to the other making a pail. When the tea leaves were barely settled she filled two tin cups. With thick slices of buttered, homemade dark bread and dark raisins sandwiched between, they enjoyed this break.

Sometimes when they had walked farther downstream than intended, it would be dusk by the time they topped the first ridge to home. Walking over rocks and across the area of grass and tussocks in the near dark, they got very close to several reindeer that had bedded down for the night. These dark forms would suddenly rise up in front of them, frightening both Minnie and her child as the animals stampeded away.

On these trips Minnie always carried a gun. Although she had never had to use it in self-defense it made her feel safer. It was always a joy to top the final rise and see the soft light from the kerosene lamp in the window of their home. Whenever they returned home before dark from berry picking, fishing, or beach-combing, which was a ten-mile walk one way, Sam would see them coming and always meet them and take Minnie's pack, carrying it the rest of the way home as they talked of the trip.

Minnie enjoyed cooking. Whenever there were supplies on hand she would make a pie or cake. She made her own yeast, so they always had homemade bread when there was flour. There were times in the spring when the sea-ice did not go out at the usual time and the boats that brought supplies could not come. Snow by then was spotty or gone, so dog teams could not travel. At this time of the year every prospector's supplies would be very low or gone, and neighbors checked with neighbors to see if they could spare what they needed. Everyone eagerly awaited the arrival of the first boat.

There being no official game regulations, any person in need of food was free to shoot ducks and geese at any time of the year, but by then most of the ducks and geese had gone further north. Hunting regulations came in later years. For a while after the seasons were established, people were allowed to shoot geese and crane with a rifle. Snipe and migratory waterfowl could also be shot with a .22 rifle. In later years only a shotgun could be used.

With the passing of time Minnie did less and less hunting. This was partly due to more regular mail boat travel between Nome and Golovin Bay. Supplies from Nome could be delivered weekly if the weather was not too stormy. She still picked berries whenever she could.

Much later a telephone line was strung from Nome to Bluff, White Mountain, Council, and other little places. Three poles, not very long, would be fastened together near the top and poles spread out at the bottom. Due to one thing or another the telephone line would often break between settlements. Someone was hired to follow the line and fix it.

About this time postal authorities decided that Bluff City no longer needed to have the word "City" added to it. Now mail would come to Bluff, via Nome, Alaska.

As time passed Minnie developed piles. Her mother also had them in later life so Minnie took it as inevitable. Since she was a rather private person she did not talk of them to Sam until they became very painful. She mentioned it to Sam just before he was to leave on the mail boat for Nome. This was a yearly trip that Sam made to deliver his summer's cleanup of gold, which he would deposit in the bank.

He also purchased supplies for the winter before returning home on the next trip. If the weather was not stormy the boat would unload the supplies on the beach in front of his home. If the sea was rough, all would be unloaded at Bluff. When it was stormy, all would be kept on the boat and taken to Golovin, with the hope the weather would be better on the way back to Nome.

On this particular trip to Nome, Sam became acquainted with one of the engineers, who once had a big problem with piles. He told Sam that after each bowel movement or whenever he felt uncomfortable he would wash off the area with seawater. When he noticed how much better he felt he kept doing it and now he hardly had any discomfort. Minnie tried doing this for awhile, but it was cumbersome carrying seawater home. She soon turned to regular water. However, the treatment seemed to have helped.

28

Heart Attack

If *someone had furs* for a parka but no money, Minnie would sew parkas and fur items for them, always doing the best job she could without asking anything in return. She took great pleasure in doing this. She said that her mother often sewed and made clothing for less fortunate people without expecting any pay in return.

Some years after their marriage, and after the big flu of 1918 which had taken so many of her relatives, Minnie thought it would be nice to spend time with her one remaining relative during the Christmas holidays. Sam decided it was probably good for her. He took her and the little children to White Mountain. Sam returned the next day because he feared many things would all be frozen if the house was left without heat for another day.

Sam arranged for her niece's husband, named Luke, to bring her home whenever she was ready. She stayed one week.

After that year Luke's wife said that he would come for Minnie on the twenty-fourth of December each year. Before the next trip Minnie baked batches of fresh bread to take.

The third year all three children stayed home with Sam because he figured such a crowd was an imposition on her relatives. Minnie returned a few days later. That year she decided to end her trips because she said she missed her family too much and wanted to be with them.

As a young adult Sam Jr. took an electrical correspondence course. The coast was usually windy. Taking advantage of it he soon designed a small windmill to charge large batteries. Now they were able to have electric lights.

Minnie's two sons each built a snow machine—one was from an old airplane engine, the other used a motorcycle engine. They wanted to try them out so they drove to White Mountain, and from there they went to Golovin, then drove home across country nearer the frozen sea.

One day when summer was nearly over the boss of the Topkok Chief Mining Company came to Sam's home and said he had a real emergency. With thirty-five men working, and the cook on a two-week leave to attend to her father's funeral, there was no one there who could take over her job. Would Sam let his daughter come over right away and cook the three meals a day, plus fix and pack a meal for the five men working the night shift? She would have no help so she must do everything, including desserts such as pies and cake. Sam recognized the gravity of this situation and also the predicament the boss was in. The boss was a good man, and both of Sam's sons were working at the mine. He agreed to let their sixteen-and-a-half-year-old daughter go if she was willing to.

Edna knew she could do the job. What to cook was another thing! She decided to attack this as if she were cooking for her family, only larger in quantities. The only help she had—which the original cook did not have—was to have the beef cut from the fresh quarter that hung in the meat shed. The boss told a reliable man that he was to cut and bring to the kitchen any cut of meat that Edna asked for each day until the regular cook returned.

Youth can accomplish amazing things. Until the regular cook returned to work, meals were always on time, the miners ate well, and they enjoyed bragging to the delivery ship's crew or anyone about the new cook's pies, to the extent that those in Nome even heard about the pies and while passing through Bluff asked about having some...but by then the regular cook was back. After working about a week, Edna walked home in the early afternoon for a short visit and to see her dog Jane and to get the fresh air and sunshine she missed. When a friend asked Minnie how her daughter was doing, Minnie said, "Her face was pale and her hands were red."

Sam and Minnie walked to Bluff on the day of the cook's father's funeral. The mining company's boss asked Edna to have coffee and refreshments in the dining room ready to serve as soon as the funeral was over, about four in the afternoon. Everything was late at the service because of the bad weather. Sam and Minnie were planning to return home, but the weather that was nasty all afternoon suddenly became much worse, turning into a real storm. The boss asked Sam and Minnie to have dinner and stay overnight. Sam could sleep in the bunkhouse with his sons and Minnie could stay with her daughter. The storm was severe. Next morning after breakfast Sam and Minnie returned home, they found that their boat had been washed away in the storm. Even if Sam had returned the evening before he could not have saved it, because he would have had to go down the steep cliff in front of the creek with no light. The extreme high wind and spray from the waves would make this too dangerous. Due to bad storms coming in the night, this was the third boat lost over the years, all made by Sam.

Before he was drafted into the armed services, Sam Jr. worked for the Topkok Chief Mining Co. during the summers. His younger brother, George, also worked for the mining company from March through summer and fall. He too was drafted into the service.

Edna took (and passed) two correspondence courses—one in taxidermy from J.W. Elwood, the other a course in writing from the Newspaper Institute of America. The *Overseas Daily Mail* in England published the first article she wrote, a short item for what they called "Your Corner of the World." She received a check for one pound eight shillings and six pence. She was also the Bluff correspondent for the Fairbanks *Daily News-Miner*, sending in brief news items. She also wrote a couple of longer articles that were published in the *Alaska Sportsman* magazine, along with photos that she had taken.

Sam and Minnie were now alone. He listened to the war news and reports of the wounded being sent home, some legless and others worse. Minnie said that it sounded very bad to Sam, and not knowing his sons' whereabouts he was very worried.

Sam suffered a heart attack. Friends sent word to Nome, where a plane was requested to take him to the hospital there.

The weather was very stormy and the pilot, Sig Wien, could not leave for a day or two. Then he took a chance during a few hours' lull in the storm and got Sam to the hospital. Edna visited him every day. Sam wanted to go home so badly but the doctor insisted he stay thirteen days. They thought he could return home then if he would take it easy for several months. He spent a day and a night at his daughter's home in Nome before returning home with Wien the next morning.

When he learned he was going to become a grandfather, Sam was very happy, and cautioned his daughter several times not to take any chances, especially while walking—he did not want her to fall or do anything that would endanger his first grandchild. Before leaving he held his daughter close and kissed her good-bye, wishing her the best for her birthday the following day.

Young Sam had been given leave and was at Bluff when Wien landed. He used a borrowed dog team to take his father home. While being bathed that evening Sam knew that he was going to die. He specifically asked Minnie and Sam Jr. to be sure to tell Edna not to come to his funeral because he did not want her to take any chance of losing his first grandchild. This said, he died before the bath was over.

There were only two men in good physical condition still living near Bluff. They came the five and seven miles and helped with the grave digging. One man who could not travel but was good at carpentry built a very nice coffin.

Word soon spread by phone and friends from White Mountain came by dog team. One, a preacher from Council, the Reverend Ost, presided over the funeral, which was held in Sam's home. Some of the elderly women stayed with Minnie for ten or more days. Young Sam, whose leave was soon to end, hastily sold as much of the household belongings as he could and gave the rest away. He moved his mother to Nome, where she could stay in a little cabin of her own. Fortunately Minnie had many friends in this town in addition to her daughter and son-in-law. Many would bring native food cooked or ready to eat and they would gather at her little cabin to eat and help her over her period of grieving.

Minnie was pleased to have a little grandson. He was named Arthur after his grandfather, and Morcom after the doctor who delivered him on the first day of June.

During Edna's stay at the hospital the Japanese invaded the Aleutian Islands, and there were many preparations around the hospital to ensure the safety of its patients. They were told that the sound of the siren would mean Nome was under attack. Women with newborn babies should get out of their beds and run down the hall, grab their babies from the nursery, and run back to their beds, climb under it, and stay there until it was safe, or they'd be destroyed. The procedure back then was for any woman who had had a baby to stay in bed for ten days before they were allowed to walk at all. After that long period of absolute inactivity, none felt as if they could get up suddenly and run down the hall.

29

"Something Terrible Would Happen"

Minnie's *son-in-law Dan decided that* since the Japanese were already on the islands, Nome was not a safe place to be because of possible Japanese bombing attacks. He got permission from the Fairbanks Mining and Exploration Company to move his family and Minnie to a little one-room cabin about twenty miles from town. He also stayed out there but continued work in town. In case of a siren alarm he would immediately drive out to the cabin, if at all possible. Fortunately that did not happen. When the fear of attacks was over they returned to Nome.

Dan, who had been sent to Nome by the F.E. Co., would complete his job by the first of September, after which he planned to return to Fairbanks with his family. He scheduled a flight to Fairbanks for the middle of the month with Wien Airlines, which was then offering one flight a week there and back.

Dan offered to take Minnie with them, but she decided to stay behind because she did not know anyone in Fairbanks, and it seemed so far away from her many friends. She wanted to stay in Nome and be there whenever her sons might visit on furlough, or better still, when they were discharged.

Packing to leave was a job. Heavy items like stoves, sewing machine, etc. were shipped to Seattle via steamship. From there they would be shipped back to Alaska, arriving in Fairbanks on the Alaska Railroad. Ten days before they were to fly to Fairbanks, Minnie's son-in-law got a premonition. He had this very urgent feeling that if they did not leave Nome before their scheduled flight "something terrible would happen." The feeling was so strong that he hurried to finish the last of the packing, and what was not ready he gave away.

Minnie hated to see them leave, but she knew that if she became too lonely she would be welcome in Fairbanks. That made waiting for her sons' return more bearable.

Later Minnie was very glad her daughter and family had left earlier than planned. The plane that they originally were to take had taken off on time. When it was about halfway to Fairbanks the propeller had fallen off and all four aboard were killed, including two who were good friends of theirs.

30

Death Is Hard

Minnie stayed in Nome waiting for her sons, who would come back on furlough for short periods. One son gave her a round-trip airplane ticket to Fairbanks. She arrived and loved seeing her grandchild and family.

Shortly after she arrived her daughter took her to town. While shopping Minnie needed to go to the bathroom. It was still wartime and sometimes there were strange restrictions or rules in place. They went to a building that had a public restroom but you had to drop a ten-cent piece into a slot before you could open the door.

"Over here you have to pay, just to do this?" a shocked Minnie exclaimed.

When the war ended both sons were honorably discharged and each decided to make his home in Nome. The youngest was married shortly after. A few years later the older son was also married. They named their first child Minnie, and another girl Violet. Minnie felt very honored to have her two names passed on.

Minnie kept thinking of her trip to Fairbanks, and decided to move there. She stayed with her daughter's family until she could find a little place to rent. Soon she was busy sewing fur pieces for the Charley Main Store, and some for individual sales.

By now her youngest son, George, and his wife had two children. He became ill with hepatitis, followed by pneumonia.

When the doctor had no hope of his recovery, word was sent to Edna.

Minnie and Edna took the next plane to Nome. George died two days later.

This death was hard on Minnie and Edna. When they returned home to Fairbanks, Dan asked Minnie to stay with them for a couple of days and rest before going back to her little rental. To make things worse, while they were in Nome, Edna's beloved dog, a yellow Labrador called "Star," had been run over and killed.

Minnie had several unfilled fur sewing orders to do, and working on these helped her to manage her grief. She sewed whenever she could. Afternoons, for a break, she often walked the two blocks to her daughter's and had tea or coffee and some homemade goodies. One day Edna, who did not have time to watch TV programs, thought her mother might like to see something different and turned on the TV. It happened to show *As the World Turns*, which interested Minnie, so she made it a point to come in time to watch that program and others that followed, occasionally staying for dinner. This also helped with her grief.

On Sundays and Wednesday evenings, Minnie would attend the Baptist church with a nice Eskimo lady called Jessie. The church provided transportation for anyone who wished to attend. (At this time Edna was not driving and had no car.)

A friend of Minnie's son-in-law, Mike Toderoff, had built several large modern rentals and decided to build a modern house for himself to enjoy in his declining years. He had been living in the first little cabin he built many years ago when he first moved to Graehl. It was not very modern but he was not used to modern conveniences. Besides, he was always too busy building new rentals. When his new house was finished, he decided to give Minnie the first chance to rent his one-room cabin.

Minnie at the woodblock keeping active. Photo by Jimmie Bedford.

It was just down the street a short ways from her daughter's. Minnie was happy to have a little house of her own, even if it was just a rental. Knowing that the landlord was a friend of her family made it even better, because she knew that he was a good man, one to be trusted.

Minnie kept active. She chopped kindling for the cookstove, baked her own bread, walked to the Market Basket to shop. Sometimes she crossed over the swinging bridge to town (Fairbanks) and shopped at Waechter's Meat Market, carrying her purchases home. When the Gavora's supermarket opened she would shop there.

She liked this little cabin with the cookstove that used either wood or coal. Her two grandsons, Arthur and Robert, were now young men. They would give her a day at the beginning of winter to chop and split wood while Edna stacked it in the shed. Sometimes men from her church, and once some young men from the service, came voluntarily to split wood and stack it. For the rest of the year her daughter did.

A white woman who lived a little beyond Minnie's cabin would often stop and talk with her on her way home. Soon Minnie and the woman became good friends. When the woman's husband retired they decided to move to the States. Both women hated to have their friendship end. Minnie missed her friend.

A month or so later Minnie was in bed one evening. She awoke before midnight but did not know what awoke her. She had a strange feeling about her friend who had left. Then she heard little footsteps coming up the street just like her friend used to make when she was returning home. These little steps stopped at Minnie's door and there was a gentle tapping sound. Then the light little footsteps continued on toward her friend's place ... all was quiet.

When Edna came by the next morning this was the first thing she told her. Next day they learned that Minnie's friend, who missed Alaska and her friends, was so excited when the mail had been delivered and, hoping to have news from Alaska, she rushed out to get the mail and was run over and killed.

31

I Just Take a Look

Minnie *would hang pictures that* she liked, including a fairly large picture of Jesus Christ, a painting of her former home by the cliffs her daughter had painted, other small pictures, and a calendar, but she had no mirror.

"No, thank you. I know what I look like, so I don't need it," was Minnie's response when someone tried to give her one.

Minnie was an early riser. After fixing the fire and putting the coffee pot on the stove she would slip into her parka and go outside for a quick look at the weather, scanning the sky before going back inside. When someone asked her why she did this, her reply would be: "They say that the Lord Jesus Christ will come back someday, so I just take a look." Back inside she would pour a cup of coffee to enjoy while the pot of old-fashioned oatmeal cooked, often frying two slices of bacon and cutting a slice or two from her home-baked bread. After saying grace she had a leisurely breakfast. She liked her coffee with a little canned milk; the oatmeal she preferred with just a little water and a light sprinkling of sugar.

One day she was out to a public event which took place at noon. Everyone had a plate of food served to them. As the people around her began to eat without saying grace, she leaned toward her daughter and in her native tongue said softly, "This will just be an extension of breakfast." Turning to her plate, she began to eat.

Over the years the minister and his wife and usually a friend or two from the church would come to her home on Wednesday or Friday, bringing a lunch to share and enjoy with her. They would sing hymns, read scriptures, and pray before leaving.

Minnie felt that her feet were bothering her more and more as the years passed. She said that they felt as if they were getting rounded on the bottom, which made it harder for her to walk and keep her balance.

One day she decided it was time to be baptized again because now she had a better understanding of what it meant. She recalled the time the missionaries first came to Golovin Bay. She had no idea why they had sprinkled her forehead with a little cold water from a container while mumbling some words that she did not understand.

She was told that at this church she would be completely immersed in water. She was to bring a towel and a dry change of clothing. Her daughter took her to church and watched her walk down the steps with the Rev. John Isaacs holding onto her arm. She stood in above-waist-high water and then, with his help, she was dipped completely underwater.

With water running off of her head she came up smiling. Her daughter had never seen her so happy and radiant. She came up the steps much more agile than when she had descended. Even before she was in dry clothes she kept saying how good she felt.

"It is like a load that has been lifted from me," she joyfully said.

While walking to the car she said that the roundness on the soles of her feet seemed to have vanished, and she felt lighter. Her good balance had returned, she could walk like a younger person again . . . she was *happy*!

When Minnie first came to Fairbanks the abundance of tall trees compared to the barren tundra she was used to made her feel almost claustrophobic. Because of the trees she could not see if a bear or any other danger might be coming. After a few years she became used to the trees. She and her son-in-law were on good terms with each other. He often invited her to go on family trips to Homer or berry picking, and once they all went out to the far hills on a caribou hunt—only problem, there was no caribou to be seen.

Maybe it was her active lifestyle or because she loved to eat fresh fish, meat, vegetables, berries or fruit, oatmeal, and whole-wheat bread, she never became overweight, remaining fit until the end.

As time passed she became used to living in Fairbanks. She enjoyed dinners with her daughter's family, especially being with the two grandsons who called her "Nana." They often made her gifts of drawings or other things that children make. Once when she was planning to go to Nome for a visit, the older grandson, Arthur, who was about six years old at the time, carved from wood what he called a spear—"Just in case she needed it for self-defense," he said.

32

Flood of '67

Minnie *was living in her* little cabin when the Great Flood of August 1967 began to flood much of Fairbanks. Just in case it continued to get worse, her son-in-law, Dan, moved her up to their home. The Chena River kept rising. After a few days it was supposed to crest that night at around 11 P.M. according to the news announcements.

Her grandson Bob and her daughter had moved their cars up to one of the higher hills near the University of Alaska. When they returned the flooding conditions were worse. Bob helped two of their nearest neighbors, Jim and Ione Couch, with his father's aluminum canoe. He took them from their home to higher ground where friends came to pick them up. The current became so strong with the fast-rising water that he was barely able to get home with the canoe. Anything in the yard that was not securely fastened was swept away. Water filled the basement and was near the first floor, which was built about four feet above ground. It was now around midnight and dark, and the news broadcasts said the flood was soon to crest.

Dan said that he would stay up and keep watch if the others cared to get some sleep. Around 1 A.M. he told them to get up and get dressed because the water was coming into the house fast.

Minnie, who had laid her dress in front of her bed, awoke to see it floating away toward the living room. Water was over a foot deep in the house by the time everyone was up.

They tried to signal passing motorized boats with the flashlight but failed time after time. Dan became worried and decided to take them all in the canoe to higher ground. First he tied a rope to it and then to the house . . . just in case. When they were all in it but still by the porch, he felt the strong current nearly tip them over. He remembered that Minnie could only dog paddle. She could not swim. With the fences all submerged in the darkness, there was a good chance that the bottom of the canoe would hit one and with the strong current it would tip the canoe—he did not want to risk it. So they all went back into the house. The floor by now had several feet of water flowing quite fast from room to room.

The four dogs—two golden retrievers and two black Labradors— were already inside. Bags of dry dog food were left open in the upstairs room and a large tub of water from the well was filled and left up there. Should they have to be left alone for a time, they would have food and water for many days. They could run downstairs if they wanted to drink the floodwater.

Dan continued to signal with a flashlight and shout at passing boats. Finally one noticed the signal and yelled that he would return and pick them up on the next trip. "Be ready to board quickly when we return," came the shouted reply.

Eventually the boat came with two men, one in charge of the motor and one to help the passengers board. He stayed in front with a light, watching for floating objects and helping to navigate.

They were taken to Bill's Service Station, which was also begin-ning to flood. They were asked to get on the back of a flatbed truck.

There they stood, crowded to the very edge, holding onto others lest they fall off. The truck drove through water nearly high enough to stall the motor; all hoped it would not as they looked at the light reflections in the water all around. They were left at Moore Hall, at the University of Alaska.

Inside each was handed a pillow and a blanket and told to go to the third floor. If there was enough space on the floor they could sleep there. In one corner they found just enough space, because so many others were already there.

Tired and finally away from the flood, Minnie heard her son-in-law exclaim as he lay down on the carpeted floor, "Oh! This feels *so* good."

Ann Hurline, who lived at Ester a few miles away, came looking for them early the next morning, bringing underclothing, hair and toothbrushes, soaps, towels, fresh fruit, and munchies.

Rumors spread that Minnie's oldest grandson, Arthur, was lost or drowned. He and his wife and children were later found—they had been sheltered in another building. A man who was seen swept away and drowned was mistaken for Arthur.

The campus was filled with the many who had been flooded out. All were thankful to the University of Alaska for opening its doors to them.

Edna helped at the cafeteria cooking, making coffee, serving food, and cleaning up after the many who had to eat. The Red Cross sent a load of clothing for those who had no change of clothes. Minnie's grandsons helped unload food brought in by the National Guard. They also worked at sandbagging, trying to keep the rising water from the University of Alaska's power plant.

During that time Minnie developed kidney stones and had to be taken to one of the military hospitals. Edna accompanied her, but after checking her mother in, she had to return on her own to the U. of A. She walked a long way before a driver, a kindly gentleman, gave her a ride to the river. From there she had to wait for a boat crossing, and then walked near the railroad tracks to the U. of A.

While Dan was spending the days waiting for the flood to recede he worried about their home and the dogs that were left. There was a warehouse on fire near their home that could be seen from the window of the building they were staying in. It added to his concern in case the fire should spread to their house, where the dogs were.

Before they could return home Dan began to feel ill. But he wouldn't go to a doctor until he could be at his home. However, their home was in a lower part of Graehl that was flooded much longer than the rest of the area. It was so damaged that the family could not live there again. Bob, using hip boots, was the first to reach the house. The dogs sounded like wild beasts when he tried to open the door but were overjoyed when they recognized him.

Minnie was discharged from the military hospital and returned to the U. of A. She too was eager and anxious to return home. But her home was a mess: the door would hardly open because the refrigerator had moved across the floor to within inches of it, the bedding was all wet and silty, chairs were here and there, some turned upside down, as was the table; pictures from her album were soaked, damaged, and spread around, and everything smelled terrible from the odoriferous floodwater.

Later, when a neighbor asked her what she missed the most from the loss of the flood, Minnie said, "My pictures... I miss my pictures." These were pictures of her family and friends, irreplaceable now because most were taken so very long ago.

Members of her church wanted to take her in but her pastor and his wife insisted she stay with them. Others from her church volunteered to clean and repair the damage, making her home livable again. For this Minnie was very thankful. Unfortunately, the man who had rented it to her had a shoulder operation and had been sent to the Sitka Pioneer Home, where he got pneumonia and died.

Dan felt worse and had to be escorted by a family friend, Chris Cotton, to Seattle for cancer treatment at the university hospital. Until the flood, Dan had been employed by the Geophysical Institute, doing top-notch drafting for twenty years.

Edna and her younger son Bob moved in with Arthur. His stove and furnace were damaged and not working so his wife and two small children did not return home from the U. of A. but took a plane back to her parents in New Jersey. They stayed until the chance of illness from the contaminated floodwater had passed and Arthur could repair the damaged stove and furnace. Everything that had been touched by the flood water smelled terrible.

Edna stopped in to see her mother every evening on her way back from out of town, where she was building a new home on much higher ground.

There were so many things to do because of all the damage to many homes and places of business. It seemed everyone was in need of material or work and few had time for the demand that came all at once. This was a very busy and trying time for Edna, who was responsible for managing her family's many affairs.

Fortunately, a friend of the family, the lawyer Sherman Noyes, came as soon as the flood was over to offer his help. It was very appreciated, for he knew where they could buy logs and land. They ordered enough three-sided logs to build a cabin.

Minnie understood why her daughter was so busy and was grateful that she took the time after a day's work with the logs to stop in to see if she needed anything before going shopping. Chores such as taking care of four dogs, going to her son's place, fixing dinner for four on the only working cookstove at the adjoining duplex, making lunches for next day, and cleaning up kept Edna busy until late at night. She and Bob would leave at five-thirty in the morning so she could start peeling logs for the day, and Bob would have Sherman's help for a few hours before he had business to attend to in town. (Dan had made this agreement with Sherman before he became too ill.)

On the first evening after working on the log house, when all other chores were finished, Edna decided to sit down in Arthur's rocker and read the paper and rest her feet, but being tired she immediately fell asleep sitting in the chair. So she stopped doing that.

During the night at this time there were some strong earthquakes that would shake the building, waking everyone.

When Minnie had moved into her little house some years earlier it was banked with mud or dirt; now this had all been washed away. Edna said, "Just wait until I get a covering on my building before it rains or snows, and I will redo it for you."

Minnie, however, decided that she could do it just as well. So with shovel in hand she went out to do just that. It had frosted in the night. While she was trying to get a shovelful of dirt she slipped and fell onto a protruding rock.

When Edna stopped by that evening, Minnie was complaining about pain in her hip. Next day Edna took her mother to the doctor. Doctors were working out of makeshift rooms and were severely limited examining patients. Minnie's doctor could not get an X-ray, but he knew by feel and pain that her hip was broken. At her age, it would be a slow recovery, and he suggested it would be best for her to go to Anchorage for an operation, and the sooner the better.

Next morning they were on a plane to Anchorage. After Minnie was checked in at the hospital, Edna had to leave, as much as she hated to. She knew that if the home was to be completed before Dan's return from the hospital, she could not stay with her mother. Already it was freezing and snow would soon follow.

33

Round Galvanized Tub

The doctor and nurses treated Minnie with kindness and respect. For a woman of her age she had an amazing range of movement. The first checkup required that she give a urine sample. The nurse gave her a container so that she would not have to leave the bed. When she got on it she looked at the three nurses who stood watching her. Minnie felt uneasy with so many eyes staring at her, waiting for her to go. After waiting awhile and the nurses were still there looking at her she said, "Do you all have to watch me do it?" They left the room, and all flowed well.

After the doctor examined her, he placed his hand on her shoulder and told her that she needed a hip operation. "At your age you may not be able to walk again after the operation," he said, pausing before continuing, "You may have to get around in a wheelchair for the rest of your life."

Minnie agreed to the operation. There was no doubt in her mind—she would walk again. She thought, *If I can walk after my broken back, I will walk after this.*

Although she had to have pins placed in her hip, the operation went well. She was told that she would be okay but should not expect to walk again after this kind of an operation, especially at her age; later, when she healed, she would be able to get around with the help of a wheelchair. Minnie did not like that idea. She did not say anything but she figured as soon as she was healed, she was walking out of this hospital. Dan was having a brain tumor removed, she wanted to see him and the rest of her family, and most of all she wanted to go back to her own home. Friends in Anchorage visited her often, bringing cards and gifts. As she healed some would bring a dish or two of her favorite food.

Eventually she was brought a walker and shown how it should be used. Minnie felt reluctant to practice with this contraption while the other patients and staff were around. So she did it during the night when things were quiet. She began to feel good about being able to get around, going further as time passed until a nurse caught her going down the hall one night. The nurse got excited when she discovered that this was "the old woman called Minnie" who was listed as unable to walk anymore. She asked Minnie how long this had been going on. Minnie told her she learned to walk because she wanted to go home and see her family and son-in-law who was sick, and that when she got home she would have to be able to walk "because I want to be back in my own home!"

The nurse told Minnie that in the morning she would get the doctors together in the next room, then have Minnie come out with her walker. Knowing how much Minnie wanted to go home she added, "Maybe then they will let you go home."

When Minnie came out using the walker, the doctors could hardly believe what they saw. Everyone cheered and clapped. Minnie was released soon after. One of her regrets was that, while she was recovering, Dan had passed away.

Minnie was released from the hospital in February, but because she still needed time to become more independent, she stayed with her daughter, who had her cabin all closed in and comfortable. Minnie wanted to go back to her little home, but she knew that with all the snow and cold it was too soon. However she was happy to be back in Fairbanks with family and friends.

During this time of recovery, she would tell her daughter about her early childhood and the way her people lived before the coming of the white man to her area. She told her daughter to write this down. "Otherwise you will forget," she said, "and the grandchildren will never know how their ancestors lived, or the hard times they experienced in order to live, without any of today's comforts." This is how and why the book *Once Upon an Eskimo Time* was written.

One day, after a good meal Minnie looked around the table at her grandchildren and said, "You know now I am glad that the white man came to this country. Before they came, there would be real hard times when the game was scarce, and when the game was scarce, everything else seemed to be gone. There would be nothing to eat. Now people are not starving to death anymore!"

Minnie made a speedy recovery. As soon as she could walk inside without a walker and needed only a walking cane when she was outdoors, she returned to her home. By then, with the increasing sunlight the weather was warm and the snow was gone.

Her daughter would stop by to see her twice a day, take her shopping if needed or shop for her if Minnie was baking or cooking. She would bring her up to her house for lunch or dinner and a regular tub bath each week. Minnie liked to have her back washed and rubbed. She also liked the modern bathtub. After years of using a round galvanized tub, this was real luxury. After about a month, before Minnie got into the tub she ran a hand around on the inside. Finding no grime, she looked at her daughter and said, "You are a good housekeeper!"

Photo of Minnie. Photographer unknown.

The pastor and his wife and other church members were very good to Minnie and would visit her and often bring meals to eat at her home. After lunch the pastor would read scriptures and pray, just as he did when she first moved to Fairbanks.

Her Eskimo friends Jessie and Elsie, who translated several hymns into Eskimo by drawing little sketches, would often come and sometimes bring a treat of special native food. The three would sing the hymns in their native tongue. Life was good again, because by now Minnie could get around quite well and it brought back memories of the days when she could walk to the Market Basket. Now she could walk to the Gavora supermarket for something light. Soon she was baking bread again.

One afternoon a man she did not recall meeting before stopped in at her place. He seated himself and then asked her if she lived alone. When she said yes, he asked her if she was ever lonely living alone. Minnie had a feeling he was not a friend.

"No," she said, as she looked up at the picture of Christ on the wall. "No, I'm never lonely, because I have Jesus for company."

He did not stay after that, just quickly said, "Well, I better go," and left.

34

Please Warn the Fisherman

Edna had been taking Minnie to church on Sundays. One Saturday evening when the temperature was still in the fifty-plus-below-zero weather Edna received a call from a former neighbor woman telling her not to come in tomorrow morning as the temperature was supposed to go to below minus fifty in the valley. "Just stay home tomorrow and I will take care of your mother, and also drive her to church."

Since the weather was so cold, it was good of the neighbor to offer. She lived just a few blocks from Minnie and had a garage so her car would be warm.

Shortly after church would have started, a call came telling Edna that there had been a car accident and that her mother was knocked unconscious and had to be removed from the neighbor's car by the Jaws of Life. She had to have thirteen stitches to the head; she was unconscious in the hospital. It seemed in the dense ice fog the neighbor and another car had crashed at an intersection.

Edna wanted to rush to the hospital, but since she had no garage and her car was not plugged in, it took more time to heat before it could be started in this extremely cold temperature.

Minnie was conscious when Edna arrived. Her mind was a little confused for a time after that. Her friend Rusty Heurlin had picked a bouquet of beautiful flowers from his garden and given them to her on her birthday, so for a time after the accident all the flowers that were given to her were from Rusty. In time her mind did return and all flowers were not from Rusty.

Since Minnie had been injured by a blow to the head, the doctor who treated her thought that she should be in a place where she could have constant care. Her daughter could not take her in because she was obligated to continue with her work in order to pay off expenses brought on by the flood: acquiring land, building a place to live, her husband's illness and death. Careage North, a nursing home, was the logical place.

It broke Edna's heart to have to move her mother there, but there seemed no alternative. She went to see her every day, sometimes two or three times a day. By summer her mother was improved enough so that Edna could take her and the wheelchair in her car. She could boost her mother into the front seat, put the folded wheelchair in the trunk, and take her to the drive-in for a treat, or bring along something Minnie liked and go out to a tiny pond nearby where there would be snipe or other birds to watch and listen to as they sat in the car with the windows open while having a picnic of sorts. Minnie loved these little trips. It brought back memories of her younger days.

For holiday meals the family would gather at Edna's home, but if some of Minnie's friends asked her early enough to come to their place, sometimes she would go there if she had promised them. Minnie always thought that if you made a promise, that promise must be kept.

As the years passed she became tired more quickly. One day Edna was gone unexpectedly for a few hours in the afternoon. She had gone with a friend's brother, who owned a small plane. They had left suddenly because the weather was good and he wanted to take her out and back before it changed. They flew to the Minto Lakes to fish for pike.

They caught their limit and were back just before dark. By the time the plane was parked and they had eaten a quick meal of fish and chips and cleaned the pike, it was too late to make her normal late-afternoon trip to see her mother. Next morning she made a point of stopping to see her mother earlier than usual. One caregiver met Edna near the door and said that her mother was so worried and upset because she had this vision of a big bird taking her daughter and flying away with her.

A mutual friend of Minnie's and Edna's would occasionally go fishing. If he was lucky he would give some or all of the fish he caught to Minnie during the time she was living in her little cabin. Minnie called him "the Fisherman." When Edna was visiting, Minnie asked her to get word to the Fisherman and warn him to be very careful the next day because something dangerous might happen to him. Edna wondered if she should do this. Her mother had seemed very serious about it, so she decided to call and tell him. There was no answer, nor was there the next day.

Later when the Fisherman returned he told of going moose hunting with a friend. They had gone by boat up one of the larger rivers. When they were trying to make a landing for the night he had slipped and fallen into the river. Fortunately his quick-thinking companion saved him from being swept away. The clothes he was wearing got wet. After they set up camp for the night they had a quick meal. His companion decided that he would check for moose in a nearby slough about a quarter of a mile away. The Fisherman would store the food, or bearproof it, and take care of his wet clothes, then join him before it got dark. Finishing his chores he hurriedly hung his clothes around the campfire, and taking his rifle he set out to join his friend. Some time after they met up a sound like a gunshot was heard from the direction of camp. Each looked at the other—they were sure that no one was within miles of where they were camped. Hurrying back they soon saw a considerable amount of smoke, more than their campfire should be making.

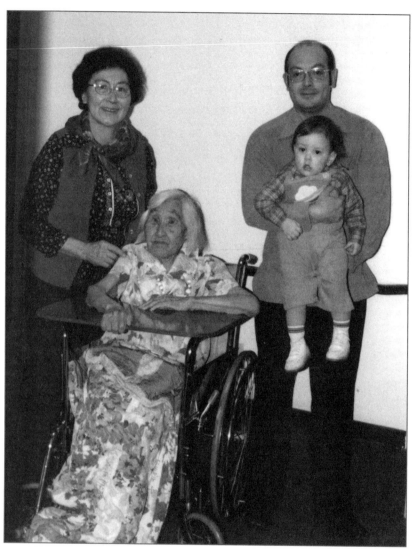

Minnie is in a wheelchair recovering from an automobile accident. Her daughter, Edna Wilder, and her grandson, Robert C. Wilder, are bringing Minnie's great-grandson, Aron D. Wilder, for a visit. Photo by Toni Wilder.

Turning a corner they saw that the tent had fallen and was ablaze. Apparently one or more of the clothes hung to dry had caught fire and was blown to the tent. It burned, along with the sleeping bags and bedding, the expensive fishing poles, and other items.

They spent the rest of the night in the dark, trying to find enough firewood to keep a fire going for light and warmth while extinguishing a smoldering spark here and there.

Thankful that the boat and gas had not burned they headed home as soon as it was light enough to run the river safely.

Talking it over later, Minnie and Edna realized that all this happened on the day that Minnie had asked her to please warn the Fisherman to be careful!

35

Man with a Heart

Since Minnie had been in a car wreck that cold, ice-foggy winter morning, she was no longer able to be physically active, and months of inactivity did not help. Edna recalled what her mother had told her years before about how she grew up in a village. Her home then was near the center of the village so there were people all around her home. After she married Sam they were only family there. If she looked in any direction she would not see anyone. She loved her family and was happy except for once in awhile. She missed the hustle and bustle about her childhood home. On one of these days Edna heard her mother praying in her native tongue. She was asking God to please let her live again in the middle of people. Her daughter thought it was ironic in a way how her prayers had been answered.

Minnie, like her mother Kiachook who had known when she was ready to take the long sleep, knew that her time was near. She had been worried about her daughter living by herself so far away from anyone, because after she had lost her home to the flood she had moved out of town.

On this day's visit Minnie was propped up in bed. Edna did not know that this would be their last conversation.

"Daughter," Minnie began, "I worry about you living out there alone. You never know...sometime there might be somebody who will come to your place who is not good. He might hurt you...you never know." She was quiet for a moment, then she continued, "If you find a good man, marry him." She rested against the pillows on her bed. "Never mind if he is not handsome or good-looking, that does not matter; neither does tall or short. What does matter, and this is the most important.... It is, if he has a HEART." As if to emphasize this she placed her hand over her heart and continued, "If you have a good man with a heart, he will take care of you."

Minnie died in her sleep that night.